I0003317

NIST Special Publication 500-288
Version 1

Specification for
WS-Biometric Devices (WS-BD)
Version 1

Recommendations of the National Institute of Standards and Technology

Ross J. Micheals
Kevin Mangold
Matt Aronoff
Kayee Kwong
Karen Marshall

INFORMATION TECHNOLOGY

Information Technology Laboratory
National Institute of Standards and Technology
Gaithersburg, MD 20899-8940

March 2012

US Department of Commerce
John E. Bryson, Secretary

National Institute of Standards and Technology
Patrick D. Gallagher, Director

The Information Technology Laboratory (ITL) at the National Institute of Standards and Technology (NIST) promotes the U.S. economy and public welfare by providing technical leadership for the nation's measurement and standards infrastructure. ITL develops tests, test methods, reference data, proof of concept implementations, and technical analysis to advance the development and productive use of information technology.

Certain commercial entities, equipment, or materials *may* be identified in this document in order to describe an experimental procedure or concept adequately. Such identification is not intended to imply recommendation or endorsement by the National Institute of Standards and Technology, nor is it intended to imply that the entities, materials, or equipment are necessarily the best available for the purpose.

Table of Contents

1   Introduction

The web services framework, has, in essence, begun to create a standard software "communications bus" in support of service-oriented architecture. Applications and services can "plug in" to the bus and begin communicating using standards tools. The emergence of this "bus" has profound implications for identity exchange.

Jamie Lewis, Burton Group, February 2005
Forward to *Digital Identity* by Phillip J. Windley

As noted by Jamie Lewis, the emergence of web services as a common communications bus has "profound implications." The next generation of biometric devices will not only need to be intelligent, secure, tamper-proof, and spoof resistant, but first, they will need to be *interoperable.*

These envisioned devices will require a communications protocol that is secure, globally connected, and free from requirements on operating systems, device drivers, form factors, and low-level communications protocols. WS-Biometric Devices is a protocol designed in the interest of furthering this goal, with a specific focus on the single process shared by all biometric systems—*acquisition*.

1.1   Request for Feedback

In the spirit of continuous improvement, feedback on this specification is both welcomed and encouraged. NIST and the authors extend an open invitation to participate in the development of this specification by sending related comments to *500-288comments@nist.gov*. This is a permanent email address; that is, it is not necessary to wait until a formal call for comments. All feedback related to content in this document will be considered as this specification is evolved and updated.

The latest version of this specification, along with related documents, can be found at *http://bws.nist.gov/*.

1.2   Terminology

This section contains terms and definitions used throughout this document. First time readers may desire to skip this section and revisit it as needed.

biometric capture device

> a system component capable of capturing biometric data in digital form

client

> a logical endpoint that originates operation requests

HTTP

> Hypertext Transfer Protocol. Unless specified, the term HTTP refers to either HTTP as defined in [RFC2616] or HTTPS as defined in [RFC2660].

ISO

> International Organization for Standardization

modality

a distinct biometric category or type of biometric—typically a short, high-level description of a human feature or behavioral characteristic (e.g., "fingerprint," "iris," "face," or "gait")

payload

the content of an HTTP request or response. An **input payload** refers to the XML content of an HTTP *request*. An **output payload** refers to the XML content of an HTTP *response.*

payload parameter

an operation parameter that is passed to a service within an input payload

profile

a list of assertions that a service *must* support

REST

Representational State Transfer

RESTful

a web service which employs REST techniques

sensor or **biometric sensor**

a single biometric capture device or a logical collection of biometric capture devices

SOAP

Simple Object Access Protocol

submodality

a distinct category or subtype within a biometric modality

target sensor or **target biometric sensor**

the biometric sensor made available by a particular service

URL parameter

a parameter passed to a web service by embedding it in the URL

Web service or **service** or **WS**

a software system designed to support interoperable machine-to-machine interaction over a network [WSGloss]

XML

Extensible Markup Language [XML]

1.3   Documentation Conventions

The following documentation conventions are used throughout this document.

1.3.1   Quotations

If the inclusion of a period within a quotation might lead to ambiguity as to whether or not the period *should* be included in the quoted material, the period will be placed outside the trailing quotation mark. For example, a sentence that ends in a quotation would have the trailing period "inside the quotation, like this quotation punctuated like this." However, a sentence that ends in a URL would have the trailing period outside the quotation mark, such as "http://example.com".

1.3.2 Machine-Readable Code

With the exception of some reference URLs, machine-readable information will typically be depicted with a mono-spaced font, such as this.

1.3.3 Sequence Diagrams

Throughout this document, sequence diagrams are used to help explain various scenarios. These diagrams are informative simplifications and are intended to help explain core specification concepts. Operations are depicted in a functional, remote procedure call style.

The following is an annotated sequence diagram that shows how an example sequence of HTTP request-responses is typically illustrated. The level of abstraction presented in the diagrams, and the details that are shown (or not shown) will vary according to the particular information being illustrated. First time readers may wish to skip this section and return to it as needed.

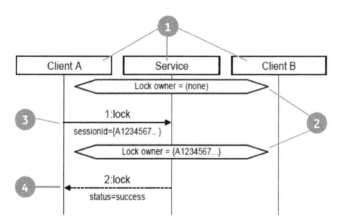

Figure 1. Example of a sequence diagram used in this document.

1. Each actor in the sequence diagram (i.e., a client or a server) has a "swimlane" that chronicles their interactions over time. Communication among the actors is depicted with arrows. In this diagram, there are three actors: "Client A," a WS-BD "Service," and "Client B."

2. State information notable to the example is depicted in an elongated diamond shape within the swimlane of the relevant actor. In this example, it is significant that the initial "lock owner" for the "Service" actor is "(none)" and that the "lock owner" changes to "{A1234567...}" after a communication from Client A.

3. Unless otherwise noted, a solid arrow represents the request (initiation) of an HTTP request; the *opening* of an HTTP socket connection and the transfer of information from a source to its destination. The arrow begins on the swimlane of the originator and ends on the swimlane of the destination. The order of the request and the operation name (§5.3 through §5.16) are shown above the arrow. URL and/or payload parameters significant to the example are shown below the arrow. In

this example, the first communication occurs when Client A opens a connection to the Service, initiating a "lock" request, where the "sessionId" parameter is "{A1234567...}."

4. Unless otherwise noted, a dotted arrow represents the response (completion) of a particular HTTP request; the *closing* of an HTTP socket connection and the transfer of information back from the destination to the source. The arrow starts on the originating request's *destination* and ends on the swimlane of actor that *originated* the request. The order of the request, and the name of the operation that being replied to is shown above the arrow. Significant data "returned" to the source is shown below the arrow (§3.11.1). Notice that the source, destination, and operation name provide the means to match the response corresponds to a particular request—there is no other visual indicator. In this example, the second communication is the response to the "lock" request, where the service returns a "status" of "success."

In general, "{A1234567...}" and "{B890B123...}" are used to represent session ids (§2.4.3, §3.11.3, §5.3); "{C1D10123...}" and "{D2E21234...}" represent capture ids (§3.11.3, §5.12).

1.4 Normative References

[CTypeImg]	*Image Media Types*, http://www.iana.org/assignments/media-types/image/index.html, 6 June 2011.
[CTypeVideo]	*Video Media Types*, http://www.iana.org/assignments/media-types/video/idex.html, 6 June 2011.
[RFC1737]	K. Sollins, L. Masinter, *Functional Requirements for Uniform Resource Names*, http://www.ietf.org/rfc/rfc1737.txt, IETC RFC 1737, December 1994.
[RFC2045]	N. Freed and N. Borenstein, *Multipurpose Internet Mail Extensions (MIME) Part One: Format of Internet Message Bodies*, http://www.ietf.org/rfc/rfc2045.txt, IETF RFC 2045, November 1996.
[RFC2046]	N. Freed and N. Borenstein, *Multipurpose Internet Mail Extensions (MIME) Part Two: Media Types*, http://www.ietf.org/rfc/rfc2046.txt, IETF RFC 2045, November 1996.
[RFC2119]	S. Bradner, *Key words for use in RFCs to Indicate Requirement Levels*, http://www.ietf.org/rfc/rfc2119.txt, IETF RFC 2119, March 1997.
[RFC2141]	R. Moats, *URN Syntax*, http://www.ietf.org/rfc/rfc2141.txt, IETF RFC 2141, May 1997
[RFC2616]	R. Fielding, et al., *Hypertext Tranfer Protocol—HTTP/1.1*, http://www.ietf.org/rfc/rfc2616.txt, IETF RFC 2616, June 1999.
[RFC2660]	E. Rescorla et al., *The Secure HyperText Transfer Protocol*, http://www.ietf.org/rfc/rfc2660.txt, IETF RFC 2660, August 1999.
[RFC3001]	M. Mealling, *A URN Namespace of Object Identifiers*, http://www.ietf.org/rfc/rfc3001.txt, IETF RFC 3001, November 2000.
[RFC4122]	P. Leach, M. Mealling, and R. Salz, *A Universally Unique Identifier (UUID) URN Namespace*, http://www.ietf.org/rfc/rfc4122.txt, IETF RFC 4122, July 2005.
[WSGloss]	H. Haas, A. Brown, *Web Services Glossary*, http://www.w3.org/TR/2004/NOTE-ws-gloss-20040211/, February 11, 2004.
[XML]	Tim Bray et al., *Extensible Markup Language (XML) 1.0 (Fifth Edition)*,

http://www.w3.org/TR/xml/. W3C Recommendation. 26 November 2008.

[XMLNS] Tim Bray et al., *Namespace in XML 1.0 (Third Edition)*, http://www.w3.org/TR/2009/REC-xml-names-20091208/. W3C Recommendation. 8 December2009.

[XSDPart1] Henry Thompson et al., *XML Schema Part 1: Structures Second Edition*, http://www.w3.org/TR/2004/REC-xmlschema-1-20041028/, W3C Recommendation. 28 October 2004.

[XSDPart2] P. Biron, A. Malhotra, *XML Schema Part 2: Datatypes Second Edition*, http://www.w3.org/TR/2004/REC-xmlschema-2-20041028/, W3C Recommendation. 28 October 2004.

1.5   Informative References

[AN2K] *Information Technology: American National Standard for Information Systems—Data Format for the Interchange of Fingerprint, Facial, & Scar Mark & Tattoo (SMT) Information*, http://www.nist.gov/customcf/get_pdf.cfm?pub_id=151453, 27 July 2000.

[AN2K7] R. McCabe, E. Newton, *Information Technology: American National Standard for Information Systems—Data Format for the Interchange of Fingerprint, Facial, & Other Biometric Information – Part 1*, http://www.nist.gov/customcf/get_pdf.cfm?pub_id=51174, 20 April 2007.

[AN2K8] E. Newton et al., *Information Technology: American National Standard for Information Systems—Data Format for the Interchange of Fingerprint, Facial, & Other Biometric Information – Part 2: XML Version*, http://www.nist.gov/customcf/get_pdf.cfm?pub_id=890062, 12 August 2008.

[AN2K11] B. Wing, *Information Technology: American National Standard for Information Systems—Data Format for the Interchange of Fingerprint, Facial & Other Biometric Information*, http://www.nist.gov/customcf/get_pdf.cfm?pub_id=910136, November 2011.

[BDIF205] ISO/IEC 19794-2:2005/Cor 1:2009/Amd 1:2010: Information technology – Biometric data interchange formats – Part 2: Finger minutia data

[BDIF306] ISO/IEC 19794-3:2006: Information technology – Biometric data interchange formats – Part 3: Finger pattern spectral data

[BDIF405] ISO/IEC 19794-4:2005: Information technology – Biometric data interchange formats – Part 4: Finger image data

[BDIF505] ISO/IEC 19794-5:2005: Information technology – Biometric data interchange formats – Part 5: Face image data

[BDIF605] ISO/IEC 19794-6:2005: Information technology – Biometric data interchange formats – Part 6: Iris image data

[BDIF611] ISO/IEC 19794-6:2011: Information technology – Biometric data interchange formats – Part 6: Iris image data

[BDIF707] ISO/IEC 19794-7:2007/Cor 1:2009: Information technology – Biometric data interchange formats – Part 7: Signature/sign time series data

[BDIF806] ISO/IEC 19794-8:2006/Cor 1:2011: Information technology – Biometric data interchange formats – Part 8: Finger pattern skeletal data

[BDIF907] ISO/IEC 19794-9:2007: Information technology – Biometric data interchange formats – Part 9: Vascular image data

[BDIF1007]	ISO/IEC 19794-10:2007: Information technology – Biometric data interchange formats – Part 10: Hand geometry silhouette data
[BMP]	*BMP File Format*, http://www.digicamsoft.com/bmp/bmp.html
[CBEFF2010]	ISO/IEC 19785-3:2007/Amd 1:2010: Information technology – Common Biometric Exchange Formats Framework – Part 3: Patron format specifications with Support for Additional Data Elements
[H264]	Y.-K. Wang et al., *RTP Payload Format for H.264 Video*, http://www.ietf.org/rfc/rfc6184.txt, IETF RFC 6184, May 2011.
[JPEG]	E. Hamilton, *JPEG File Interchange Format*, http://www.w3.org/Graphics/JPEG/jfif3.pdf, 1 September 1992.
[MPEG]	ISO/IEC 14496: Information technology – Coding of audio-visual objects
[PNG]	D. Duce et al., *Portable Network Graphics (PNG) Specification (Second Edition)*, http://www.w3.org/TR/2003/REC-PNG-20031110, 10 November 2003.
[TIFF]	*TIFF Revision 6.0*, http://partners.adobe.com/public/developer/en/tiff/TIFF6.pdf, 3 June 1992.
[WSQ]	*WSQ Gray-Scale Fingerprint Image Compression Specification Version 3.1*, https://fbibiospecs.org/docs/WSQ_Gray-scale_Specification_Version_3_1_Final.pdf, 4 October 2010.

2   Design Concepts and Architecture

This section describes the major design concepts and overall architecture of WS-BD. The main purpose of a WS-BD service is to expose a target biometric sensor to clients via web services.

This specification provides a framework for deploying and invoking core synchronous operations via lightweight web service protocols for the command and control of biometric sensors. The design of this specification is influenced heavily by the REST architecture; deviations and tradeoffs were made to accommodate the inherent mismatches between the REST design goals and the limitations of devices that are (typically) oriented for a single-user.

2.1   Interoperability

ISO/IEC 2382-1 (1993) defines *interoperability* as *"the capability to communicate, execute programs, or transfer data among various functional units in a manner that requires the user to have little to no knowledge of the unique characteristics of those units."*

Conformance to a standard does not necessarily guarantee interoperability. An example is conformance to an HTML specification. A HTML page may be fully conformant to the HTML 4.0 specification, but it is not interoperable between web browsers. Each browser has its own interpretation of how the content *should* be displayed. To overcome this, web developers add a note suggesting which web browsers are compatible for viewing. Interoperable web pages need to have the same visual outcome independent of which browser is used.

A major design goal of WS-BD is to *maximize* interoperability, by *minimizing* the required "knowledge of the unique characteristics" of a component that supports WS-BD. The authors recognize that conformance to this specification alone cannot guarantee interoperability; although a minimum degree of functionality is implied. Sensor *profiles* and accompanying conformance tests will need to be developed to provide better guarantees of interoperability, and will be released in the future.

2.2   Architectural Components

Before discussing the envisioned use of WS-BD, it is useful to distinguish between the various components that comprise a WS-BD implementation. These are *logical* components that may or may not correspond to particular *physical* boundaries. This distinction becomes vital in understanding WS-BD's operational models.

2.2.1   Client

A *client* is any software component that originates requests for biometric acquisition. Note that a client might be one of many hosted in a parent (logical or physical) component, and that a client might send requests to a variety of destinations.

 This icon is used to depict an arbitrary WS-BD client. A personal digital assistant (PDA) is used to serve as a reminder that a client might be hosted on a non-traditional computer.

2.2.2   Sensor

A biometric *sensor* is any component that is capable of acquiring a digital biometric sample. Most sensor components are hosted within a dedicated hardware component, but this is not necessarily globally true. For example, a keyboard is a general input device, but might also be used for a keystroke dynamics biometric.

 This icon is used to depict a biometric sensor. The icon has a vague similarity to a fingerprint scanner, but *should* be thought of as an arbitrary biometric sensor.

The term "sensor" is used in this document in a singular sense, but may in fact be referring to multiple biometric capture devices. Because the term "sensor" may have different interpretations, practitioners are encouraged to detail the physical and logical boundaries that define a "sensor" for their given context.

2.2.3   Sensor Service

The *sensor service* is the "middleware" software component that exposes a biometric sensor to a client through web services. The sensor service adapts HTTP request-response operations to biometric sensor command & control.

 This icon is used to depict a sensor service. The icon is abstract and has no meaningful form, just as a sensor service is a piece of software that has no physical form.

2.3   Intended Use

Each implementation of WS-BD will be realized via a mapping of logical to physical components. A distinguishing characteristic of an implementation will be the physical location of the sensor service component. WS-BD is designed to support two scenarios:

1. **Physically separated.** The sensor service and biometric sensor are hosted by different physical components. A *physically separated service* is one where there is both a physical and logical separation between the biometric sensor and the service that provides access to it.
2. **Physically integrated.** The sensor service and biometric sensor are hosted within the same physical component. A *physically integrated service* is one where the biometric sensor and the service that provides access to it reside within the same physical component.

Figure 2 depicts a physically separated service. In this scenario, a biometric sensor is tethered to a personal computer, workstation, or server. The web service, hosted on the computer, listens for communication requests from clients. An example of such an implementation would be a USB fingerprint scanner attached to a personal computer. A lightweight web service, running on that computer could listen to requests from local (or remote) clients—translating WS-BD requests to and from biometric sensor commands.

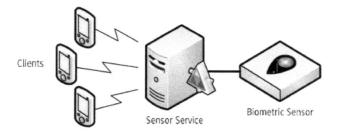

Figure 2. A physically separated WS-Biometric Devices (WS-BD) implementation.

Figure 3 depicts a physically integrated service. In this scenario, a single hardware device has an embedded biometric sensor, as well as a web service. Analogous (but not identical) functionality is seen in many network printers; it is possible to point a web browser to a local network address, and obtain a web page that displays information about the state of the printer, such as toner and paper levels (WS-BD enabled devices do not provide web pages to a browser). Clients make requests directly to the integrated device; and a web service running within an embedded system translates the WS-BD requests to and from biometric sensor commands.

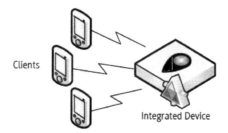

Figure 3. A physically integrated WS-Biometric Devices (WS-BD) implementation.

The "separated" versus "integrated" distinction is a simplification with a potential for ambiguity. For example, one might imagine putting a hardware shell around a USB fingerprint sensor connected to a small form-factor computer. Inside the shell, the sensor service and sensor are on different physical components. Outside the shell, the sensor service and sensor appear integrated. Logical encapsulations, i.e., layers of abstraction, can facilitate analogous "hiding". The definition of what constitutes the "same" physical component depends on the particular implementation and the intended level of abstraction. Regardless, it is a useful distinction in that it illustrates the flexibility afforded by leveraging highly interoperable communications protocols. As suggested in §2.2.2, practitioners *may* need to clearly define appropriate logical and physical boundaries for their own context of use.

2.4   General Service Behavior

The following section describes the general behavior of WS-BD clients and services.

2.4.1   Security Model

In this version of the specification, it is assumed that if a client is able to establish an HTTP (or HTTPS) connection with the sensor service, then the client is fully authorized to use the service. This implies that all successfully connected clients have equivalent access to the same service. Clients might be required to connect through various HTTP protocols, such as HTTPS with client-side certificates, or a more sophisticated protocol such as Open Id (http://openid.net/) and/or OAuth.

Specific security measures are out of scope of this specification, but *should* be carefully considered when implementing a WS-BD service. Some recommended solutions to general scenarios are outlined in the following sections.

2.4.1.1   Development

During initial development stages, security *may* not be a concern—focusing on the design and implementation of a high fidelity service *may* be the primary concern. Security measures shall be integrated before deployment in a production environment.

2.4.1.2   Isolated Network

An isolated network is one where services running in such network are not accessible outside of a particular subnet or domain. These restrictions could be enforced by firewalls, network address translation (NAT), or by simply not being connected to an external network.

At minimum, the use of HTTP over a SSL/TLS connection, more commonly known as HTTPS, *should* be implemented to secure communication between a service and any connected clients.

2.4.1.3   Publicly Accessibility

This scenario is where a service or services are accessible from any subnet or domain. In other words, anyone from any location could access the service.

Mutual authentication *should* be implemented. Mutual authentication, or two-way authentication, is when two parties authenticate themselves to each other. In other words, the client authenticates to the server via a client-side certificate and validates the server by its server-side certificate. Any communication shall be through HTTP over a mutual SSL/TLS connection.

2.4.2   HTTP Request-Response Usage

Most biometrics devices are inherently *single user*—i.e., they are designed to sample the biometrics from a single user at a given time. Web services, on the other hand, are intended for *stateless* and *multiuser* use. A biometric device exposed via web services *must* therefore provide a mechanism to reconcile these competing viewpoints.

Notwithstanding the native limits of the underlying web server, WS-BD services *must* be capable of handling multiple, concurrent requests. Services *must* respond to requests for operations that do not require exclusive control of the biometric sensor and *must* do so without waiting until the biometric sensor is in a particular state.

Because there is no well-accepted mechanism for providing asynchronous notification via REST, each individual operation *must* block until completion. That is, the web server does not reply to an individual HTTP request until the operation that is triggered by that request is finished.

Individual clients are not expected to poll—rather they make a single HTTP request and block for the corresponding result. Because of this, it is expected that a client would perform WS-BD operations on an independent thread, so not to interfere with the general responsiveness of the client application. WS-BD clients therefore *must* be configured in such a manner such that individual HTTP operations have timeouts that are compatible with a particular implementation.

WS-BD operations may be longer than typical REST services. Consequently, there is a clear need to differentiate between service level errors and HTTP communication errors. WS-BD services *must* pass-through the status codes underlying a particular request. In other words, services *must not* use (or otherwise 'piggyback') HTTP status codes to indicate failures that occur within the service. If a service successfully receives a well-formed request, then the service *must* return the HTTP status code 200 indicating such. Failures are described within the contents of the XML data returned to the client for any given operation. The exception to this is when the service receives a poorly-formed request (i.e., the XML payload is not valid), then the service *may* return the HTTP status code 400, indicating a bad request.

This is deliberately different from REST services that override HTTP status codes to provide service-specific error messages. Avoiding the overloading of status codes is a pattern that facilitates the debugging and troubleshooting of communication versus client & service failures.

> **DESIGN NOTE**: Overriding HTTP status codes is just one example of the rich set of features afforded by HTTP; content negotiation, entity tags (e-tags), and preconditions are other features that could be leveraged instead of "recreated" (to some degree) within this specification. However, the authors avoided the use of these advanced HTTP features in this version of the specification for several reasons:
>
> - To reduce the overall complexity required for implementation.
> - To ease the requirements on clients and servers (particularly since the HTTP capabilities on embedded systems may be limited).
> - To avoid dependencies on any HTTP feature that is not required (such as entity tags).
>
> In summary, the goal for this initial version of the specification is to provide common functionality across the broadest set of platforms. As this standard evolves, the authors will continue to evaluate the integration of more advanced HTTP features, as well as welcome feedback on their use from users and/or implementers of the specification.

2.4.3   Client Identity

Before discussing how WS-BD balances single-user vs. multi-user needs, it is necessary to understand the WS-BD model for how an individual client can easily and consistently identify itself to a service.

HTTP is, by design, a *stateless* protocol. Therefore, any persistence about the originator of a sequence of requests *must* be built in (somewhat) artificially to the layer of abstraction above HTTP itself. This is accomplished in WS-BD via a *session*—a collection of operations that originate from the same logical endpoint. To initiate a session, a client performs a *registration* operation and obtains a *session identifier* (or "session id"). During subsequent operations, a client uses this identifier as a parameter to uniquely identify itself to a server. When the client is finished, it is expected to close a session with an *unregistration* operation. To conserve resources, services *may* automatically unregister clients that do not explicitly unregister after a period of inactivity (see §5.4.2.1).

This use of a session id directly implies that the particular sequences that constitute a session are entirely the responsibility of the *client*. A client might opt to create a single session for its entire lifetime, or, might open (and close) a session for a limited sequence of operations. WS-BD supports both scenarios.

It is possible, but discouraged, to implement a client with multiple sessions with the same service simultaneously. For simplicity, and unless otherwise stated, this specification is written in a manner that assumes that a single client maintains a single session id. (This can be assumed without loss of generality, since a client with multiple sessions to a service could be decomposed into "sub-clients"—one sub- client per session id.)

Just as a client might maintain multiple session ids, a single session id might be shared among a collection of clients. By sharing the session id, a biometric sensor may then be put in a particular state by one client, and then handed-off to another client. This specification does not provide guidance on how to perform multi-client collaboration. However, session id sharing is certainly permitted, and a deliberate artifact of the convention of using of the session id as the client identifier. Likewise, many-to-many relationships (i.e., multiple session ids being shared among multiple clients) are also possible, but *should* be avoided.

2.4.4   Sensor Identity

In general, implementers *should* map each target biometric sensor to a single endpoint (URI). However, just as it is possible for a client to communicate with multiple services, a host might be responsible for controlling multiple target biometric sensors.

Independent sensors *should* be exposed via different URIs.

> **EXAMPLE:** Figure 4 shows a physically separate implementation where a single host machine controls two biometric sensors—one fingerprint scanner and one digital camera. The devices act independently and are therefore exposed via two different services—one at the URL *http://wsbd/fingerprint* and one at *http://wsbd/camera*.

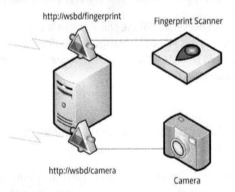

Figure 4. Independent sensors controlled by separate services

A service that controls multiple biometric devices simultaneously (e.g., an array of cameras with synchronized capture) *should* be exposed via the same endpoint.

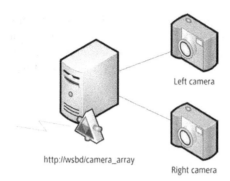

Figure 5. A sensor array controlled by a single service

EXAMPLE: Figure 5 shows a physically separate implementation where a single host machine controls a pair of cameras used for stereo vision. The cameras act together as a single logical sensor and are both exposed via the same service, `http://wsbd/camera_array`.

2.4.5   Locking

WS-BD uses a *lock* to satisfy two complementary requirements:

1. A service *must* have exclusive, sovereign control over biometric sensor hardware to perform a particular *sensor operation* such as initialization, configuration, or capture.
2. A client needs to perform an uninterrupted sequence of sensor operations.

Each WS-BD service exposes a *single* lock (one per service) that controls access to the sensor. Clients obtain the lock in order to perform a sequence of operations that *should not* be interrupted. Obtaining the lock is an indication to the server (and indirectly to peer clients) that (1) a series of sensor operations is about to be initiated and (2) that server *may* assume sovereign control of the biometric sensor.

A client releases the lock upon completion of its desired sequence of tasks. This indicates to the server (and indirectly to peer clients) that the uninterruptable sequence of operations is finished. A client might obtain and release the lock many times within the same session or a client might open and close a session for each pair of lock/unlock operations. This decision is entirely dependent on a particular client.

The statement that a client might "own" or "hold" a lock is a convenient simplification that makes it easier to understand the client-server interaction. In reality, each sensor service maintains a unique global variable that contains a session id. The originator of that session id can be thought of as the client that "holds" the lock to the service. Clients are expected to release the lock after completing their required sensor operations, but there is lock *stealing*—a mechanism for forcefully releasing locks. This feature is necessary to ensure that one client cannot hold a lock indefinitely, denying its peers access to the biometric sensor.

As stated previously (see §2.4.3), it is implied that all successfully connected clients enjoy the same access privileges. Each client is treated the same and are expected to work cooperatively with each other. This is critically important, because it is this implied equivalence of "trust" that affords a lock *stealing* operation.

DESIGN NOTE: In the early development states of this specification, the authors considered having a single, atomic sensor operation that performed initialization, configuration *and* capture. This would avoid the need for locks entirely, since a client could then be ensured (if successful), the desired operation completed as requested. However, given the high degree of variability of sensor operations across different sensors and modalities, the explicit locking was selected so that clients could have a higher degree of control over a service and a more reliable way to predict timing. Regardless of the enforcement mechanism, it is undesirable if once a "well-behaved" client started an operation and a "rogue" client changed the internal state of the sensor midstream.

2.4.5.1 Pending Operations

Changing the state of the lock *must* have no effect on pending (i.e., currently running) sensor operations. That is, a client *may* unlock, steal, or even re-obtain the service lock even if the target biometric sensor is busy. When lock ownership is transferred during a sensor operation, overlapping sensor operations are prevented by sensor operations returning `sensorBusy`.

2.4.6   Operations Summary

All WS-BD operations fall into one of eight categories:

1. Registration
2. Locking
3. Information
4. Initialization
5. Configuration
6. Capture
7. Download
8. Cancellation

Of these, the initialization, configuration, capture, and cancellation operations are all sensor operations (i.e., they require exclusive sensor control) and require locking. Registration, locking, and download are all non-sensor operations. They do not require locking and (as stated earlier) *must* be available to clients regardless of the status of the biometric sensor.

Download is not a sensor operation as this allows for a collection of clients to dynamically share acquired biometric data. One client might perform the capture and hand off the download responsibility to a peer.

The following is a brief summary of each type of operation:

- *Registration* operations open and close (unregister) a session.
- *Locking* operations are used by a client to obtain the lock, release the lock, and *steal* the lock.
- *Information* operations query the service for information about the service itself, such as the supported biometric modalities, and service configuration parameters.
- The *initialization* operation prepares the biometric sensor for operation.
- *Configuration* operations get or set sensor parameters.
- The *capture* operation signals to the sensor to acquire a biometric.
- *Download* operations transfer the captured biometric data from the service to the client.
- Sensor operations can be stopped by the *cancellation* operation.

2.4.7 Idempotency

The W3C Web Services glossary [WSGloss] defines idempotency as:

> *[the] property of an interaction whose results and side-effects are the same whether it is done one or multiple times.*

When regarding an operation's idempotence, it *should* be assumed no *other* operations occur in between successive operations, and that each operation is successful. Notice that idempotent operations may have side-effects—but the final state of the service *must* be the same over multiple (uninterrupted) invocations.

The following example illustrates idempotency using an imaginary web service.

> **EXAMPLE**: A REST-based web service allows clients to create, read, update, and delete customer records from a database. A client executes an operation to update a customer's address from "123 Main St" to "100 Broad Way."
>
> Suppose the operation is idempotent. Before the operation, the address is "123 Main St". After one execution of the update, the server returns "success", and the address is "100 Broad Way". If the operation is executed a second time, the server again returns "success," and the address remains "100 Broad Way".
>
> Now suppose that when the operation is executed a second time, instead of returning "success", the server returns "no update made", since the address was already "100 Broad Way." Such an operation is *not* idempotent, because executing the operation a second time yielded a different result than the first execution.

The following is an example in the context of WS-BD.

> **EXAMPLE**: A service has an available lock. A client invokes the lock operation and obtains a "success" result. A subsequent invocation of the operation also returns a "success" result. The operation being idempotent means that the results ("success") and side-effects (a locked service) of the two sequential operations are identical.

To best support robust communications, WS-BD is designed to offer idempotent services whenever possible.

2.4.8   Service Lifecycle Behavior

The lifecycle of a service (i.e., when the service starts responding to requests, stops, or is otherwise unavailable) *must* be modeled after an integrated implementation. This is because it is significantly easier for a physically separated implementation to emulate the behavior of a fully integrated implementation than it is the other way around. This requirement has a direct effect on the expected behavior of how a physically separated service would handle a change in the target biometric sensor.

Specifically, on a desktop computer, hot-swapping the target biometric sensor is possible through an operating system's plug-and-play architecture. By design, this specification does not assume that it is possible to replace a biometric sensor within an integrated device. Therefore, having a physically separated implementation emulate an integrated implementation provides a simple means of providing a common level of functionality.

By virtue of the stateless nature of the HTTP protocol, a client has no simple means of detecting if a web service has been restarted. For most web communications, a client *should not* require this—it is a core capability that constitutes the robustness of the web. Between successive web requests, a web server might be restarted on its host any number of times. In the case of WS-BD, replacing an integrated device with another (configured to respond on the same endpoint) is an *effective* restart of the service. Therefore, by the emulation requirement, replacing the device within a physically separated implementation *must* behave similarly.

A client may not be directly affected by a service restart, if the service is written in a robust manner. For example, upon detecting a new target biometric sensor, a robust server could *quiesce* (refusing all new requests until any pending requests are completed) and automatically restart.

Upon restarting, services *should* return to a fully reset state—i.e., all sessions *should* be dropped, and the lock *should not* have an owner. However, a high-availability service *may* have a mechanism to preserve state across restarts, but is significantly more complex to implement (particularly when using integrated implementations!). A client that communicated with a service that was restarted would lose both its session and the service lock (if held). With the exception of the *get service info* operation, through various fault statuses a client would receive indirect notification of a service restart. If needed, a client could use the service's common info timestamp (§A.1.1) to detect potential changes in the *get service info* operation.

3   Data Dictionary

This section contains descriptions of the data elements that are contained within the WS-BD data model. Each data type is described via an accompanying XML Schema type definition [XSDPart1, XSDPart2].

Refer to Appendix A for a complete XML schema containing all types defined in this specification.

3.1   Namespaces

The following namespaces, and corresponding namespace prefixes are used throughout this document.

Prefix	Namespace	Remarks
xs	http://www.w3.org/2001/XMLSchema	The xs namespace refers to the XML Schema specification. Definitions for the xs data types (i.e., those not explicitly defined here) can be found in [XSDPart2].
xsi	http://www.w3.org/2001/XMLSchema-instance	The xsi namespace allows the schema to refer to other XML schemas in a qualified way.
wsbd	urn:oid:2.16.840.1.101.3.9.3.1	The wsbd namespace is a uniform resource name [RFC1737, RFC2141] consisting of an object identifier [RFC3001] reserved for this specification's schema. This namespace can be written in ASN.1 notation as {joint-iso-ccitt(2) country(16) us(840) organization(1) gov(101) csor(3) biometrics(9) wsbd(3) version1(1)}.

All of the datatypes defined in this section (§3) belong to the wsbd namespace defined in the above table. If a datatype is described in the document without a namespace prefix, the wsbd prefix is assumed.

3.2   UUID

A UUID is a unique identifier as defined in [RFC4122]. A service *must* use UUIDs that conform to the following XML Schema type definition.

```
<xs:simpleType name="UUID">
  <xs:restriction base="xs:string">
    <xs:pattern value="[\da-fA-F]{8}-[\da-fA-F]{4}-[\da-fA-F]{4}-[\da-fA-F]{4}-[\da-fA-F]{12}"/>
  </xs:restriction>
</xs:simpleType>
```

EXAMPLE: Each of the following code fragments contains a well-formed UUID. Enclosing tags (which may vary) are omitted.

```
E47991C3-CA4F-406A-8167-53121C0237BA
```

```
10fa0553-9b59-4D9e-bbcd-8D209e8d6818
```

```
161FdBf5-047F-456a-8373-D5A410aE4595
```

3.3   Dictionary

A Dictionary is a generic container used to hold an arbitrary collection of name-value pairs.

```
<xs:complexType name="Dictionary">
  <xs:sequence>
    <xs:element name="item" minOccurs="0" maxOccurs="unbounded">
      <xs:complexType>
        <xs:sequence>
          <xs:element name="key" type="xs:string" nillable="true"/>
          <xs:element name="value" type="xs:anyType" nillable="true"/>
        </xs:sequence>
      </xs:complexType>
    </xs:element>
  </xs:sequence>
</xs:complexType>
```

EXAMPLE: A query to get the metadata of a capture returns a dictionary of supported settings and the values at the time of capture. Enclosing tags (which may vary) are omitted.

```
<item>
  <key>imageWidth</key>
  <value>640</value>
</item>
<item>
  <key>imageHeight</key>
  <value>640</value>
</item>
<item>
  <key>captureDate</key>
  <value>2011-01-01T01:23:45Z</value>
</item>
```

Dictionary instances are nestable—i.e., the value element of one Dictionary can contain another Dictionary. The use of xs:anyType allows for an XML element of any structure or definition to be used. Using types not defined in this document or types defined in W3's XML Schema recommendations [**XSDPart1, XSDPart2**] might require a client to have unique knowledge about the service. Because the requirement of unique knowledge negatively impacts interoperability, using such elements is discouraged.

3.4   Parameter

A Parameter is a container used to describe the parameters or settings of a service or sensor.

```
<xs:complexType name="Parameter">
  <xs:sequence>
    <xs:element name="name" type="xs:string" nillable="true"/>
    <xs:element name="type" type="xs:QName" nillable="true"/>
    <xs:element name="readOnly" type="xs:boolean" minOccurs="0"/>
    <xs:element name="supportsMultiple" type="xs:boolean" minOccurs="0"/>
    <xs:element name="defaultValue" type="xs:anyType" nillable="true"/>
    <xs:element name="allowedValues" nillable="true" minOccurs="0">
      <xs:complexType>
        <xs:sequence>
          <xs:element name="allowedValue" type="xs:anyType" nillable="true" minOccurs="0"
maxOccurs="unbounded"/>
        </xs:sequence>
```

```
        </xs:complexType>
      </xs:element>
    </xs:sequence>
  </xs:complexType>
```

See §4 for more information on metadata and the use of Parameter.

3.4.1.1 Element Summary

The following is a brief informative description of each Parameter element.

Element	Description
name	The name of the parameter.
type	The fully qualified type of the parameter.
readOnly	Whether or not this parameter is read-only.
supportsMultiple	Whether or not this parameter can support multiple values for this parameter (§3.4.1.2).
defaultValue	The default value of this parameter.
allowedValues	A list of allowed values for this parameter (§3.4.1.3).

3.4.1.2 Supports Multiple

In some cases, a parameter might require multiple values. This flag specifies whether the parameter is capable of multiple values.

When supportsMultiple is true, communicating values must be done through a defined array type. If a type-specialized array is defined in this specification, such as a StringArray (§3.7) for xs:string, such type *should* be used. The generic Array (§3.6) type *must* be used in all other cases.

The parameter's type element *must* be the qualified name of a single value. For example, if the parameter expects multiple strings during configuration, then the type *must* be xs:string and not StringArray.

EXAMPLE: An iris scanner might have the ability to capture a left iris, right iris, and/or frontal face image simultaneously. This example configures the scanner to capture left and right iris images together. The first code block is what the service exposes to the clients. The second code block is how a client would configure this parameter. The client configures the submodality by supplying a StringArray with two elements: left and right—this tells the service to capture both the left and right iris. It is important to note that in this example, submodality exposes values for two modalities: iris and face. The resulting captured data *must* specify the respective modality for each captured item in its metadata. In both examples, enclosing tags (which may vary) are omitted.

```
<name>submodality</name>
<type>xs:string</type>
<readOnly>false</readOnly>
<supportsMultiple>true</supportsMultiple>
<defaultValue xsi:type="wsbd:StringArray">
  <element>leftIris</element>
  <element>rightIris</element>
</defaultValue>
<allowedValues>
  <allowedValue>leftIris</allowedValue>
  <allowedValue>rightIris</allowedValue>
```

```
  <allowedValue>frontalFace</allowedValue>
</allowedValues>
```

```
<item>
  <key>submodality</key>
  <value xsi:type="wsbd:StringArray">
    <element>leftIris</element>
    <element>rightIris</element>
  </value>
</item>
```

3.4.1.3 Allowed Values

For parameters that are not read-only and have restrictions on what values it may have, this allows the service to dynamically expose it to its clients.

EXAMPLE: The following code block demonstrates a parameter, "CameraFlash", with only three valid values. Enclosing tags (which may vary) are omitted.

```
<name>cameraFlash</name>
<type>xs:string</type>
<readOnly>false</readOnly>
<supportsMultiple>false</supportsMultiple>
<defaultValue>auto</defaultValue>
<allowedValues>
  <allowedValue xsi:type="xs:string">on</allowedValue>
  <allowedValue xsi:type="xs:string">off</allowedValue>
  <allowedValue xsi:type="xs:string">auto</allowedValue>
</allowedValues>
```

Parameters requiring a range of values *should* be described by using Range (§3.5). Because the allowed type is not the same as its parameter type, a service *must* have logic to check for a Range and any appropriate validation.

EXAMPLE: The following code block demonstrates a parameter, "CameraZoom", where the allowed value is of type Range and consists of integers. Enclosing tags (which may vary) are omitted.

```
<name>cameraZoom</name>
<type>xs:integer</type>
<readOnly>false</readOnly>
<supportsMultiple>false</supportsMultiple>
<defaultValue>0</defaultValue>
<allowedValues>
  <allowedValue xsi:type="wsbd:Range">
    <minimum>0</minimum>
    <maximum>100</maximum>
  </allowedValue>
</allowedValues>
```

Configurable parameters with no restrictions on its value *must not* include this element.

3.5 Range

A Range is a container used to describe a range of data, and whether the upper and lower bounds are exclusive. The upper and lower bounds *must* be inclusive by default.

```
<xs:complexType name="Range">
```

```
<xs:sequence>
  <xs:element name="minimum" type="xs:anyType" nillable="true" minOccurs="0"/>
  <xs:element name="maximum" type="xs:anyType" nillable="true" minOccurs="0"/>
  <xs:element name="minimumIsExclusive" type="xs:boolean" nillable="true" minOccurs="0"/>
    <xs:element name="maximumIsExclusive" type="xs:boolean" nillable="true" minOccurs="0"/>
</xs:sequence>
</xs:complexType>
```

EXAMPLE: An example range of numbers from 0 to 100. The minimum is exclusive while the maximum is inclusive. Enclosing tags (which may vary) are omitted.

```
<minimum>0</minimum>
<maximum>100</maximum>
<minimumIsExclusive>true</minimumIsExclusive>
<maximumIsExclusive>false</maximumIsExclusive>
```

3.5.1.1 Element Summary

The following is a brief informative description of each Range element.

Element	Description
minimum	The lower bound of the range.
maximum	The upper bound of the range.
minimumIsExclusive	Boolean indicating whether the lower bound is exclusive or not. This is true by default.
maximumIsExclusive	Boolean indicating whether the upper bound is exclusive or not. This is true by default.

3.6   Array

An Array is a generic container used to hold a collection of elements.

```
<xs:complexType name="Array">
  <xs:sequence>
    <xs:element name="element" type="xs:anyType" nillable="true" minOccurs="0"
maxOccurs="unbounded"/>
  </xs:sequence>
</xs:complexType>
```

EXAMPLE: Each of the following code fragments is an example of a valid Array. Enclosing tags (which may vary) are omitted.

```
<element>flatLeftThumb</element><element>flatRightThumb</element>
```

In this fragment (above), the values "flatLeftThumb" and "flatRightThumb" are of type xs:anyType, (and are likely to be deserialized as a generic "object."

```
<element xsi:type="xs:boolean">false</element><element xsi:type="xs:int">1024</element>
```

Notice that in this fragment (above) the two values are of *different* types

```
<element xsi:type="xs:decimal">2.0</element>
```

In this fragment (above) the array contains a single element.

3.7   StringArray

A StringArray is a generic container used to hold a collection of strings.

```
<xs:complexType name="StringArray">
  <xs:sequence>
    <xs:element name="element" type="xs:string" nillable="true" minOccurs="0"
maxOccurs="unbounded"/>
  </xs:sequence>
</xs:complexType>
```

EXAMPLE: Each of the following code fragments is an example of a valid StringArray. Enclosing tags (which may vary) are omitted.

```
<element>flatLeftThumb</element><element>flatRightThumb</element>
```

```
<element>value1</element><element>value2</element>
```

```
<element>sessionId</element>
```

3.8   UuidArray

A UuidArray is a generic container used to hold a collection of UUIDs.

```
<xs:complexType name="UuidArray">
  <xs:sequence>
    <xs:element name="element" type="wsbd:UUID" nillable="true" minOccurs="0"
maxOccurs="unbounded"/>
  </xs:sequence>
</xs:complexType>
```

EXAMPLE: The following code fragment is an example of a *single* UuidArray with three elements. Enclosing tags (which may vary) are omitted.

```
<element>E47991C3-CA4F-406A-8167-53121C0237BA</element>
<element>10fa0553-9b59-4D9e-bbcd-8D209e8d6818</element>
<element>161FdBf5-047F-456a-8373-D5A410aE4595</element>
```

3.9   Resolution

Resolution is a generic container to describe values for a width and height and optionally a description of the unit.

```
<xs:complexType name="Resolution">
  <xs:sequence>
    <xs:element name="width" type="xs:decimal"/>
    <xs:element name="height" type="xs:decimal"/>
    <xs:element name="unit" type="xs:string" nillable="true" minOccurs="0"/>
  </xs:sequence>
</xs:complexType>
```

3.9.1.1 Element Summary

The following is a brief informative description of each Size element.

Element	Description
width	The decimal value of the width
height	The decimal value of the height
unit	A string describing the units of the width and height values

3.10 Status

The Status represents a common enumeration for communicating state information about a service.

```
<xs:simpleType name="Status">
  <xs:restriction base="xs:string">
    <xs:enumeration value="success"/>
    <xs:enumeration value="failure"/>
    <xs:enumeration value="invalidId"/>
    <xs:enumeration value="canceled"/>
    <xs:enumeration value="canceledWithSensorFailure"/>
    <xs:enumeration value="sensorFailure"/>
    <xs:enumeration value="lockNotHeld"/>
    <xs:enumeration value="lockHeldByAnother"/>
    <xs:enumeration value="initializationNeeded"/>
    <xs:enumeration value="configurationNeeded"/>
    <xs:enumeration value="sensorBusy"/>
    <xs:enumeration value="sensorTimeout"/>
    <xs:enumeration value="unsupported"/>
    <xs:enumeration value="badValue"/>
    <xs:enumeration value="noSuchParamter"/>
    <xs:enumeration value="preparingDownload"/>
  </xs:restriction>
</xs:simpleType>
```

3.10.1.1 Definitions

The following table defines all of the potential values for the Status enumeration.

Value	Description
success	The operation completed successfully.
failure	The operation failed. The failure was due to a web service (as opposed to a sensor error).
invalidId	The provided id is not valid. This can occur if the client provides a (session or capture) id that is either:
	unknown to the server (i.e., does not correspond to a known registration or capture result), or
	the session has been closed by the service (§5.4.2.1)
	(See §5.1.2 for information on parameter failures.)
canceled	The operation was canceled.
	NOTE: A sensor service *may* cancel its own operation, for example, if an operation is taking too long. This can happen if a service maintains its own

	internal timeout that is shorter than a sensor timeout.
canceledWithSensorFailure	The operation was canceled, but during (and perhaps because of) cancellation, a sensor failure occurred. This particular status accommodates for hardware that may not natively support cancellation.
sensorFailure	The operation could not be performed because of a biometric sensor (as opposed to web service) failure. NOTE: Clients that receive a status of `sensorFailure` should assume that the sensor will need to be reinitialized in order to restore normal operation.
lockNotHeld	The operation could not be performed because the client does not hold the lock. NOTE: This status implies that at the time the lock was queried, no other client currently held the lock. However, this is not a guarantee that any subsequent attempts to obtain the lock will succeed.
lockHeldByAnother	The operation could not be performed because another client currently holds the lock.
initializationNeeded	The operation could not be performed because the sensor requires initialization.
configurationNeeded	The operation could not be performed because the sensor requires configuration.
sensorBusy	The operation could not be performed because the sensor is currently performing another task. NOTE: Services *may* self-initiate an activity that triggers a sensorBusy result. That is, it may not be possible for a client to trace back a sensorBusy status to any particular operation. An automated self-check, heartbeat, or other activity such as a data transfer *may* place the target biometric sensor into a "busy" mode. (See §5.13.2.2 for information about post-acquisition processing.)
sensorTimeout	The operation was not performed because the biometric sensor experienced a timeout. NOTE: The most common cause of a sensor timeout would be a lack of interaction with a sensor within an expected timeframe.
unsupported	The service does not support the requested operation. (See §5.1.2 for information on parameter failures.)
badValue	The operation could not be performed because a value provided for a particular parameter was either (a) an incompatible type or (b) outside of an acceptable range. (See §5.1.2 for information on parameter failures.)
noSuchParameter	The operation could not be performed because the service did not recognize the name of a provided parameter. (See §5.1.2 for information on parameter failures.)

> *preparingDownload*   The operation could not be performed because the service is currently preparing captured data for download. (See §5.13.2.2)

Many of the permitted status values have been designed specifically to support physically separate implementations—a scenario where it is easier to distinguish between failures in the web service and failures in the biometric sensor. This is not to say that within an integrated implementation such a distinction is not possible, only that some of the status values are more relevant for physically separate versions.

For example, a robust service would allow all sensor operations to be canceled with no threat of a failure. Unfortunately, not all commercial, off-the-shelf (COTS) sensors natively support cancellation. Therefore, the *canceledWithSensorFailure* status is offered to accommodate this. Implementers can still offer cancellation, but have a mechanism to communicate back to the client that sensor initialization might be required.

3.11 Result

Unless a service returns with an HTTP error, all WS-BD operations *must* reply with an HTTP message that contains an element of a Result type that conforms to the following XML Schema snippet.

```
<xs:element name="result" type="wsbd:Result" nillable="true"/>

<xs:complexType name="Result">
  <xs:sequence>
    <xs:element name="status" type="wsbd:Status"/>
    <xs:element name="badFields" type="wsbd:StringArray" nillable="true" minOccurs="0"/>
    <xs:element name="captureIds" type="wsbd:UuidArray" nillable="true" minOccurs="0"/>
    <xs:element name="metadata" type="wsbd:Dictionary" nillable="true" minOccurs="0"/>
    <xs:element name="message" type="xs:string" nillable="true" minOccurs="0"/>
    <xs:element name="sensorData" type="xs:base64Binary" nillable="true" minOccurs="0"/>
    <xs:element name="sessionId" type="wsbd:UUID" nillable="true" minOccurs="0"/>
  </xs:sequence>
</xs:complexType>
```

3.11.1 Terminology Shorthand

Since a Result is the intended outcome of all requests, this document *may* state that an operation "returns" a particular status value. This is shorthand for a Result output payload with a `status` element containing that value.

EXAMPLE: The following result payload "returns `success`". A result might contain other child elements depending on the specific operation and result status—see §1 for operations and their respective details.

```
<result xmlns="urn:oid:2.16.840.1.101.3.9.3.1"
        xmlns:xs="http://www.w3.org/2001/XMLSchema"
        xmlns:xsi="http://www.w3.org/2001/XMLSchema-instance">
  <status>success</status>
</result>
```

Likewise, the same shorthand is implied by a client "receiving" a status, or an operation "yielding" a status.

3.11.2 Required Elements

Notice that from a XML Schema validation perspective [XSDPart1], a schema-valid Result *must* contain a `status` element, and may contain any of the remaining elements.

The specific permitted elements of a Result are determined via a combination of (a) the operation, and (b) the result's status. That is, different operations will have different requirements on which elements are permitted or forbidden, depending on that operation's status.

> **EXAMPLE**: As will be detailed later (§5.3.4.1 and §5.5.4.1), a _register_ operation returning a status of success _must_ also populate the sessionId element. However, a _try lock_ operation that returns a status of success cannot populate any element other than status.

DESIGN NOTE: An XML inheritance hierarchy could have been used to help enforce which elements are permitted under which circumstances. However, a de-normalized representation (in which all of the possible elements are valid with respect to a _schema_) was used to simplify client and server implementation. Further, this reduces the burden of managing an object hierarchy for the sake of enforcing simple constraints.

3.11.3 Element Summary

The following is a brief informative description of each Result element.

Element	Description
status	The disposition of the operation. All Result elements _must_ contain a status element. (Used in all operations.)
badFields	The list of fields that contain invalid or ill-formed values. (Used in almost all operations.)
captureIds	Identifiers that _may_ be used to obtain data acquired from a capture operation (§5.12, §5.13).
metadata	This field _may_ hold a) metadata for the service (§5.8), or b) a service and sensor's configuration (§5.10, §5.11), or c) metadata relating to a particular capture (§5.13, §5.14, §5.15) (See §4 for more information regarding metadata)
message	A string providing _informative_ detail regarding the output of an operation. (Used in almost all operations.)
sensorData	The biometric data corresponding to a particular capture identifier (§5.13, §5.15).
sessionId	A unique session identifier (§5.3).

3.12 Validation

The provided XML schemas _may_ be used for initial XML validation. It should be noted that these are not strict schema definitions and were designed for easy consumption of web service/code generation tools. Additional logic _should_ be used to evaluate the contents and validity of the data where the schema falls short. For example, additional logic will be necessary to verify the contents of a Result are accurate as there is not a different schema definition for every combination of optional and mandatory fields.

A service _must_ have separate logic validating parameters and their values during configuration. The type of any allowed values might not correspond with the type of the parameter. For example, if the type of the parameter is an integer and an allowed value is a Range, the service *must* handle this within the service as it cannot be appropriately validated using XML schema.

4   Metadata

Metadata can be broken down into three smaller categories: service information, sensor information or configuration, and capture information. Metadata can be returned in two forms: as a key/value pair within a Dictionary or a Dictionary of Parameter types.

4.1   Service Information

Service information includes read-only parameters unrelated to the sensor as well as parameters that can be set. Updating the values of a parameter *should* be done in the set configuration operation.

Service information *must* include the required parameters listed in Appendix A; including the optional parameters is highly recommended. Each parameter *must* be exposed as a Parameter (§3.4).

Parameters listed in §A.1, §A.2, and §A.3 *must* be exposed as read-only parameters.

Read-only parameters *must* specify its current value by populating the default value field with the value. Additionally, read-only parameters *must not* provide any allowed values. Allowed values are reserved to specify acceptable information which *may* be passed *to* the service for configuration.

EXAMPLE: An example snippet from a *get service info* call demonstrating a read-only parameter. Enclosing tags (which may vary) are omitted.

```
<name>inactivityTimeout</name>
<type>xs:nonNegativeInteger</type>
<readOnly>true</readOnly>
<supportsMultiple>false</supportsMultiple>
<defaultValue>600</defaultValue>
```

Configurable parameters, or those which are not read only, *must* provide information for the default value as well as allowed values. To specify that an allowed value is within range of numbers, refer to Range (§3.5).

EXAMPLE: An example snippet from a *get service info* call. The target service supports a configurable parameter called "ImageWidth". Enclosing tags (which may vary) are omitted.

```
<name>imageWidth</name>
<type>xs:positiveInteger</type>
<readOnly>false</readOnly>
<supportsMultiple>false</supportsMultiple>
<defaultValue>800</defaultValue>
<allowedValues>
  <allowedValue>640</allowedValue>
  <allowedValue>800</allowedValue>
  <allowedValue>1024</allowedValue>
</allowedValues>
```

In many cases, an exposed parameter will support multiple values (see §3.4.1.2). When a parameter allows this capability, it *must* use a type-specific array, if defined in this specification, or the generic `Array` (§3.6) type. The `type` element within a parameter *must* be the qualified name of a single value's type (see §3.4.1.2 for an example).

4.2   Configuration

A configuration consists of parameters specific to the sensor or post-processing related to the final capture result. This *must* only consist of key/value pairs. It *must not* include other information about the parameters, such as allowed values or read-only status.

Restrictions for each configuration parameter can be discovered through the *get service info* operation.

EXAMPLE: The following is an example payload to *set configuration* consisting of three parameters.

```
<configuration xmlns="urn:oid:2.16.840.1.101.3.9.3.1"
               xmlns:xs="http://www.w3.org/2001/XMLSchema"
               xmlns:xsi="http://www.w3.org/2001/XMLSchema-instance">
  <item>
    <key>imageHeight</key>
    <value xsi:type="xs:int">480</value>
  </item>
  <item>
    <key>imageWidth</key>
    <value xsi:type="xs:int">640</value>
  </item>
  <item>
    <key>frameRate</key>
    <value xsi:type="xs:int">20</value>
  </item>
</configuration>
```

4.3   Captured Data

Metadata related to a particular capture operation *must* include the configuration of the sensor at the time of capture. Static parameters related to the service *should not* be included in the metadata for a capture result.

A service *may* perform post-processing steps on any captured information. This information *should* be added to the particular capture result's metadata.

EXAMPLE: Example metadata for a particular capture. Note that this includes parameters related to the sensor. Enclosing tags (which may vary) are omitted.

```
<item>
  <key>serialNumber</key>
  <value xsi:type="xs:string">98A8N830LP332-V244</value>
</item>
<item>
  <key>imageHeight</key>
  <value xsi:type="xs:string">600</value>
</item>
<item>
  <key>imageWidth</key>
  <value xsi:type="xs:string">800</value>
</item>
<item>
  <key>captureTime</key>
  <value xsi:type="xs:dateTime">2011-12-02T09:39:10.935-05:00</value>
```

```
</item>
<item>
  <key>contentType</key>
  <value xsi:type="xs:string">image/jpeg</value>
</item>
<item>
  <key>modality</key>
  <value xsi:type="xs:string">Finger</value>
</item>
<item>
  <key>submodality</key>
  <value xsi:type="xs:string">LeftIndex</value>
</item>
```

EXAMPLE: A service computes the quality score of a captured fingerprint (see previous example). This score is added to the result's metadata to allow other clients to take advantage of previously completed processes. Enclosing tags (which may vary) are omitted.

```
<item>
  <key>quality</key>
  <value>78</value>
</item>
<item>
  <key>serialNumber</key>
  <value>98A8N830LP332-V244</value>
</item>
<item>
  <key>captureDate</key>
  <value>2011-01-01T15:30:00Z</value>
</item>
<item>
  <key>modality</key>
  <value>Finger</value>
</item>
<item>
  <key>submodality</key>
  <value>leftIndex</value>
</item>
<item>
  <key>imageHeight</key>
  <value>600</value>
</item>
<item>
  <key>imageWidth</key>
  <value>800</value>
</item>
<item>
  <key>contentType</key>
  <value>image/bmp</value>
</item>
```

4.3.1 Minimal Metadata

At a minimum, a sensor or service *must* maintain the following metadata fields for each captured result.

4.3.1.1 Capture Date

    Formal Name   captureDate

       Data Type   xs:dateTime [XSDPart2]

This value represents the date and time at which the capture occurred.

4.3.1.2   Modality

Formal Name	modality
Data Type	xs:string [XSDPart2]

The value of this field *must* be present in the list of available modalities exposed by the *get service info* operation (§5.8) as defined in §A.4.1. This value represents the modality of the captured result.

4.3.1.3   Submodality

Formal Name	submodality
Data Type	xs:anyType [XSDPart2]

The value of this field *must* be present in the list of available submodalities exposed by the *get service info* operation (§5.8) as defined in §A.4.2. This value represents the submodality of the captured result. If this parameter supports multiple, then the data type *must* be a StringArray (§3.7) of values. If submodality does not support multiple, the data type *must* be xs:string [XSDPart2].

4.3.1.4   Content Type

Formal Name	contentType
Data Type	xs:string [RFC2045, RFC2046]

The value of this field represents the content type of the captured data. See Appendix A for which content types are supported.

5   Operations

This section provides detailed information regarding each WS-BD operation.

5.1   General Usage Notes

The following usage notes apply to all operations, unless the detailed documentation for a particular operation conflicts with these general notes, in which case the detailed documentation takes precedence.

1. **Failure messages are informative.** If an operation fails, then the message element *may* contain an informative message regarding the nature of that failure. The message is for informational purposes only—the functionality of a client *must not* depend on the contents of the message.

2. **Results *must* only contain required and optional elements.** Services *must* only return elements that are either required or optional. All other elements *must not* be contained in the result, even if they are empty elements. Likewise, to maintain robustness in the face of a non-conformant service, clients *should* ignore any element that is not in the list of permitted Result elements for a particular operation call.

3. **Sensor operations *must not* occur within a non-sensor operation.** Services *should only* perform any sensor control within the operations:
    a. *initialize*,
    b. *get configuration*,
    c. *set configuration*,
    d. *capture*, and
    e. *cancel*.

4. **Sensor operations *must* require locking.** Even if a service implements a sensor operation without controlling the target biometric sensor, the service *must* require that a locked service for the operation to be performed.

5. **Content Type.** Clients *must* make HTTP requests using a content type of `application/xml` [RFC2616, §14].

6. **Namespace.** A data type without an explicit namespace or namespace prefix implies it is a member of the `wsbd` namespace as defined in §3.1.

5.1.1   Precedence of Status Enumerations

To maximize the amount of information given to a client when an error is obtained, and to prevent different implementations from exhibiting different behaviors, all WS-BD services *must* return status values according to a fixed priority. In other words, when multiple status messages might apply, a higher-priority status *must* always be returned in favor of a lower-priority status.

The status priority, listed from highest priority (`"invalidId"`) to lowest priority (`"success"`) is as follows:

1. `invalidId`
2. `noSuchParameter`
3. `badValue`
4. `unsupported`
5. `canceledWithSensorFailure`
6. `canceled`

```
 7.  lockHeldByAnother
 8.  lockNotHeld
 9.  sensorBusy
10.  sensorFailure
11.  sensorTimeout
12.  initializationNeeded
13.  configurationNeeded
14.  preparingDownload
15.  failure
16.  success
```

Notice that success is the *lowest* priority—an operation *should* only be deemed successful if no *other* kinds of (non-successful) statuses apply.

The following example illustrates how this ordering affects the status returned in a situation in which multiple clients are performing operations.

EXAMPLE: Figure 6 illustrates that client cannot receive a "sensorBusy" status if it does not hold the lock, even if a sensor operation is in progress (recall from §2.4.5 that sensor operations require holding the lock). Suppose there are two clients; Client A and Client B. Client A holds the lock and starts initialization on (Step 1–3). Immediately after Client A initiates capture, Client B (Step 4) tries to obtain the lock while Client A is still capturing. In this situation, the valid statuses that could be returned to Client B are "sensorBusy" (since the sensor is busy performing a capture) and "lockHeldByAnother" (since Client A holds the lock). In this case, the service returns "lockHeldByAnother" (Step 5) since "lockHeldByAnother" is higher priority than "sensorBusy."

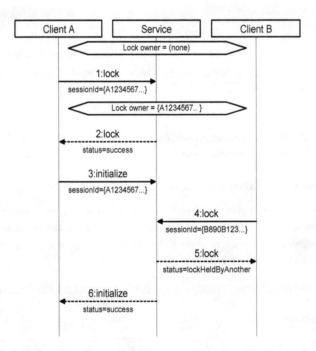

Figure 6. Example illustrating how a client cannot receive a "sensorBusy" status if it does not hold the lock.

5.1.2   Parameter Failures

Services *must* distinguish among `badValue`, `invalidId`, `noSuchParameter`, and `unsupported` according to the following rules. These rules are presented here in the order of precedence that matches the previous subsection.

1.   **Is a recognizable UUID provided?** If the operation requires a UUID as an input URL parameter, and provided value is not an UUID (i.e., the UUID is *not* parseable), then the service *must* return `badValue`. Additionally, the Result's `badFields` list *must* contain the name of the offending parameter (`sessionId` or `captureId`).

     ...otherwise...

2.   **Is the UUID understood?** If an operation requires an UUID as an input URL parameter, and the provided value *is* a UUID, but service cannot accept the provided value, then the service *must* return `invalidId`. Additionally, the Result's `badFields` list *must* contain the name of the offending parameter (`sessionId` or `captureId`).

     ...otherwise...

3.   **Are the parameter names understood?** If an operation does not recognize a provided input parameter *name*, then the service *must* return `noSuchParameter`. This behavior *may* differ from service to service, as different services *may* recognize (or not recognize) different parameters. The unrecognized parameter(s) *must* be listed in the Result's `badFields` list.

     ...otherwise...

4.   **Are the parameter values acceptable?** If an operation recognizes all of the provided parameter names, but cannot accept a provided *value* because it is (a) and inappropriate type, or (b) outside the range advertised by the service (§4.1), the then service *must* return `badValue`. The parameter names associated with the unacceptable values *must* be listed in the Result's `badFields` list. Clients are expected to recover the bad values themselves by reconciling the Result corresponding to the offending request.

     ...otherwise...

5.   **Is the request supported?** If an operation accepts the parameter names and values, but the particular request is not supported by the service or the target biometric sensor, then the service *must* return `unsupported`. The parameter names that triggered this determination *must* be listed in the Result's `badFields` list. By returning multiple fields, a service is able to imply that a particular *combination* of provided values is unsupported.

NOTE: It may be helpful to think of `invalidId` as a special case of `badValue` reserved for URL parameters of type UUID.

5.1.3   Visual Summaries

The following two tables provide *informative* visual summaries of WS-BD operations. These visual summaries are an overview; they are not authoritative. (§5.3–5.16 are authoritative.)

5.1.3.1   Input & Output

The following table represents a visual summary of the inputs and outputs corresponding to each operation.

Operation *inputs* are indicated in the "URL Fragment" and "Input Payload" columns. Operation inputs take the form of either (a) a URL parameter, with the parameter name shown in "curly brackets" ("{" and "}") within the URL fragment (first column), and/or, (b) a input payload (defined in §1.2).

Operation *outputs* are provided via Result, which is contained in the body of an operation's HTTP response.

Summary of Operations Input/Output												
						Permitted Result Elements (within output payload)						
Operation	**URL Fragment (Includes inputs)**	**Method**	**Input payload**	**Idempotent**	**Sensor Operation**	**status**	**badFields**	**sessionId**	**metadata**	**captureIds**	**sensorData**	**Detailed Documentation (§)**
register	/register	POST	none			●		●				5.3
unregister	/register/{sessionId}	DELETE	none	◆		●	●	●				5.4
try lock		POST	none	◆		●	●					5.5
steal lock	/lock/{sessionId}	PUT	none	◆		●	●					5.6
unlock		DELETE	none	◆		●	●	●				5.7
get service info	/info	GET	none	◆		●			●			5.8
initialize	/initialize/{sessionId}	POST	none	◆	■	●	●					5.9
get configuration	/configure/{sessionId}	GET	none	◆	■	●	●		●			5.10
set configuration	/configure/{sessionId}	POST	config	◆	■	●	●					5.11
capture	/capture/{sessionId}	POST	none		■	●	●			●		5.12
download	/download/{captureId}	GET	none	◆		●	●		●		●	5.13
get download info	/download/{captureId}/info	GET	none	◆		●			●			5.14
thrifty download	/download/{captureId}/{maxSize}	GET	none	◆		●	●		●		●	5.15
cancel operation	/cancel/{sessionId}	POST	none	◆	■	●	●					5.16

Presence of a symbol in a table cell indicates that operation is idempotent (◆), a sensor operation (■), and which elements may be present in the operation's Result (●). Likewise, the lack of a symbol in a table cell indicates the operation is not idempotent, not a sensor operation, and which elements of the operation's Result are forbidden.

> **EXAMPLE**: The *capture* operation (fifth row from the bottom) is not idempotent, but is a sensor operation. The output *may* contain the elements status, badFields, and/or captureIds in its Result. The detailed information regarding the Result for *capture*, (i.e., which elements are specifically permitted under what circumstances) is found in §5.12.

The message element is not shown in this table for two reasons. First, when it appears, it is *always* optional. Second, to emphasize that the message content *must* only be used for informative purposes; it *must not* be used as a vehicle for providing unique information that would inhibit a service's interoperability.

5.1.3.2 Permitted Status Values

The following table provides a visual summary of the status values permitted.

Possible Status Values Per Operation																
Operation Description \ **Status Values**	success	failure	invalidId	canceled	canceledWithSensorFailure	sensorFailure	lockNotHeld	lockHeldByAnother	initializationNeeded	configurationNeeded	sensorBusy	sensorTimeout	unsupported	badValue	noSuchParameter	preparingDownload
register	●	●														
unregister	●	●	●								●			●		
try lock	●	●	●					●						●		
steal lock	●	●	●											●		
unlock	●	●	●					●						●		
get service info	●	●														
initialize	●	●	●	●	●	●	●	●			●	●		●		
get configuration	●	●	●	●	●	●	●	●	●	●	●	●		●		
set configuration	●	●	●	●	●	●	●	●	●		●	●	●	●	●	
capture	●	●	●	●	●	●	●	●	●		●	●		●		
download	●	●	●											●		●
get download info	●	●	●											●		●
thrifty download	●	●	●										●	●		●
cancel	●	●	●			●	●							●		

The presence (absence) of a symbol in a cell indicates that the respective status *may* (*may not*) be returned by the corresponding operation.

> **EXAMPLE**: The *register* operation *may* only return a Result with a Status that contains either success or failure. The *unregister* operation *may* only return success, failure, invalidId, sensorBusy, or badValue.

The visual summary does not imply that services may return these values arbitrarily—the services *must* adhere to the behaviors as specified in their respective sections.

5.2   Documentation Conventions

Each WS-BD operation is documented according to the following conventions.

5.2.1   General Information

Each operation begins with the following tabular summary:

Description	A short description of the operation

URL Template	The suffix used to access the operation. These take the form
	
	`/resourceName`
	
	or
	
	`/resourceName/{URL_parameter_1}/…/{URL_parameter_N}`
	
	Each parameter, `{URL_parameter...}` *must* be replaced, in-line with that parameter's value.
	
	Parameters have no explicit names, other than defined by this document or reported back to the client within the contents of a `badFields` element.
	
	It is assumed that consumers of the service will prepend the URL to the service endpoint as appropriate.
	
	EXAMPLE: The resource `resourceName` hosted at the endpoint
	
	`http://example.com/Service`
	
	would be accessible via
	
	`http://example.com/Service/resourceName`

HTTP Method	The HTTP method that triggers the operation, i.e., `GET`, `POST`, `PUT`, or `DELETE`
URL Parameters	A description of the URL-embedded operation parameters. For each parameter the following details are provided: • the name of the parameter • the expected data type (§1) • a description of the parameter
Input Payload	A description of the content, if any, to be posted to the service as input to an operation.
Idempotent	Yes—the operation is idempotent (§2.4.7). No—the operation is not idempotent.
Sensor Operation (Lock Required)	Yes—the service *may* require exclusive control over the target biometric sensor. No—this operation does not require a lock. Given the concurrency model (§2.4.5) this value doubles as documentation as to whether or not a lock is required

5.2.2   Result Summary

This subsection summarizes the various forms of a Result that *may* be returned by the operation. Each row represents a distinct combination of permitted values & elements associated with a particular status. An operation that returns `success` *may* also provide additional information other than `status`.

`success`	`status="success"`
`failure`	`status="failure"`
	`message*=`informative message describing failure
`[status value]`	status=status literal
	[required element name]=description of permitted contents of the element
	[optional element name]*=description of permitted contents of the element
⋮	⋮

For each row, the left column contains a permitted status value, and the right column contains a summary of the constraints on the Result when the `status` element takes that specific value. The vertical ellipses at the bottom of the table signify that the summary table may have additional rows that summarize other permitted status values.

Data types without an explicit namespace or namespace prefix are members of the `wsbd` namespace as defined in §3.1.

Element names suffixed with a '*' indicate that the element is *optional*.

5.2.3   Usage Notes

Each of the following subsections describes behaviors & requirements that are specific to its respective operation.

5.2.4   Unique Knowledge

For each operation, there is a brief description of whether or not the operation affords an opportunity for the server or client to exchange information unique to a particular implementation. The term "unique knowledge" is used to reflect the definition of interoperability referenced in §2.1.

5.2.5   Return Values Detail

This subsection details the various return values that the operation *may* return. For each permitted status value, the following table details the Result requirements:

Status Value	The particular status value
Condition	The service accepts the registration request
Required Elements	A list of the required elements. For each required element, the element name, its expected contents, and expected data type is listed If no namespace prefix is specified, then the `wsbd` namespace (§3.1) is inferred.
	For example, `badFields={"sessionId"}` (StringArray, §3.7)

	Indicates that `badFields` is a required element, and that the contents of the element *must* be a wsbd:StringArray containing the single literal `"sessionId"`.
Optional Elements	A list of the required elements. Listed for each optional element are the element names and its expected contents.

Constraints and information unique to the particular operation/status combination may follow the table, but some status values have no trailing explanatory text.

A data type without an explicit namespace or namespace prefix implies it is a member of the `wsbd` namespace as defined in §3.1.

5.3   Register

Description	Open a new client-server session
URL Template	/register
HTTP Method	POST
URL Parameters	None
Input Payload	None
Idempotent	No
Sensor Operation	No

5.3.1   Result Summary

success	status="success"
	sessionId=session id (UUID, §3.2)
failure	status="failure"
	message*=informative message describing failure

5.3.2   Usage Notes

Register provides a unique identifier that can be used to associate a particular client with a server. In a sequence of operations with a service, a *register* operation is likely one of the first operations performed by a client (*get service info* being the other). It is expected (but not required) that a client would perform a single registration during that client's lifetime.

DESIGN NOTE: By using an UUID, as opposed to the source IP address, a server can distinguish among clients sharing the same originating IP address (i.e., multiple clients on a single machine, or multiple machines behind a firewall). Additionally, a UUID allows a client (or collection of clients) to determine client identity rather than enforcing a particular model (§2.4.3).

5.3.3   Unique Knowledge

As specified, the *register* operation cannot be used to provide or obtain knowledge about unique characteristics of a client or service.

5.3.4   Return Values Detail

The *register* operation *must* return a Result according to the following constraints.

5.3.4.1   Success

Status Value	success
Condition	The service accepts the registration request
Required Elements	status (Status, §3.10)
	the literal "success"
	sessionId (UUID, §3.2)

	an identifier that can be used to identify a session
Optional Elements	None

The "register" operation *must not* provide a `sessionId` of 00000000-0000-0000-0000-000000000000.

5.3.4.2　Failure

Status Value	`failure`
Condition	The service cannot accept the registration request
Required Elements	`status` (Status, §3.10) the literal "`failure`"
Optional Elements	`message` (xs:string, [XSDPart2]) an informative description of the nature of the failure

Registration might fail if there are too many sessions already registered with a service. The `message` element *must* only be used for informational purposes. Clients *must not* depend on particular contents of the message element to control client behavior.

See §4 and §A.1 for how a client can use sensor metadata to determine the maximum number of current sessions a service can support.

5.4   Unregister

Description	Close a client-server session
URL Template	/register/{sessionId}
HTTP Method	DELETE
URL Parameters	{sessionId} (UUID, §3.2) Identity of the session to remove
Input Payload	None
Idempotent	Yes
Sensor Operation	No

5.4.1   Result Summary

success	status="success"
failure	status="failure" message*=informative message describing failure
sensorBusy	status="sensorBusy"
badValue	status="badValue" badFields={"sessionId"} (StringArray, §3.7)

5.4.2   Usage Notes

Unregister closes a client-server session. Although not strictly necessary, clients _should_ unregister from a service when it is no longer needed. Given the lightweight nature of sessions, services _should_ support (on the order of) thousands of concurrent sessions, but this cannot be guaranteed, particularly if the service is running within limited computational resources. Conversely, clients _should_ assume that the number of concurrent sessions that a service can support is limited. (See §A.1 for details on connection metadata.)

5.4.2.1   Inactivity
A service _may_ automatically unregister a client after a period of inactivity, or if demand on the service requires that least-recently used sessions be dropped. This is manifested by a client receiving a status of invalidId without a corresponding unregistration. Services _should_ set the inactivity timeout to a value specified in minutes. (See §A.1 for details on connection metadata.)

5.4.2.2   Sharing Session Ids
A session id is not a secret, but clients that share session ids run the risk of having their session prematurely terminated by a rogue peer client. This behavior is permitted, but discouraged. See §2.4 for more information about client identity and the assumed security models.

5.4.2.3   Locks & Pending Sensor Operations
If a client that holds the service lock unregisters, then a service _must_ also release the service lock, with one exception. If the unregistering client both holds the lock and is responsible for a pending sensor operation, the service _must_ return sensorBusy (See §5.4.4.3).

5.4.3   Unique Knowledge

As specified, the *unregister* operation cannot be used to provide or obtain knowledge about unique characteristics of a client or service.

5.4.4   Return Values Detail

The *unregister* operation *must* return a Result according to the following constraints.

5.4.4.1   Success

Status Value	success
Condition	The service accepted the unregistration request
Required Elements	status (Status, §3.10) the literal "success"
Optional Elements	None

If the unregistering client currently holds the service lock, and the requesting client is not responsible for any pending sensor operation, then successful unregistration *must* also release the service lock.

As a consequence of idempotency, a session id does not need to ever have been registered successfully in order to *un*register successfully. Consequently, the *unregister* operation cannot return a status of invalidId.

5.4.4.2   Failure

Status Value	failure
Condition	The service could not unregister the session.
Required Elements	status (Status, §3.10) the literal "failure"
Optional Elements	message (xs:string, [XSDPart2]) an informative description of the nature of the failure

In practice, failure to unregister is expected to be a rare occurrence. Failure to unregister might occur if the service experiences a fault with an external system (such as a centralized database used to track session registration and unregistration)

5.4.4.3   Sensor Busy

Status Value	sensorBusy
Condition	The service could not unregister the session because the biometric sensor is currently performing a sensor operation within the session being unregistered.
Required Elements	status (Status, §3.10) the literal "sensorBusy"
Optional Elements	None

This status *must* only be returned if (a) the sensor is busy and (b) the client making the request holds the lock (i.e., the session id provided matches that associated with the current service lock). Any client that does not hold the session lock *must not* result in a sensorBusy status.

EXAMPLE: The following sequence diagram illustrates a client that cannot unregister (Client A) and a client that can unregister (Client B). After the initialize operation completes (Step 6), Client A can unregister (Steps 7-8).

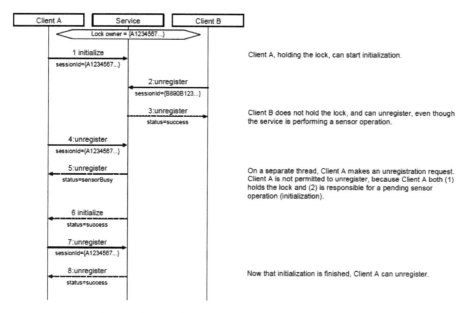

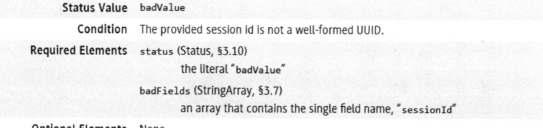

Figure 7. Example of how an *unregister* operation can result in `sensorBusy`.

5.4.4.4 Bad Value

Status Value	`badValue`
Condition	The provided session id is not a well-formed UUID.
Required Elements	`status` (Status, §3.10) the literal "`badValue`" `badFields` (StringArray, §3.7) an array that contains the single field name, "`sessionId`"
Optional Elements	None

See §5.1.2 for general information on how services *must* handle parameter failures.

5.5 Try Lock

Description	Try to obtain the service lock
URL Template	/lock/{sessionId}
HTTP Method	POST
URL Parameters	{sessionId} (UUID, §3.2)
	Identity of the session requesting the service lock
Input Payload	None
Idempotent	Yes
Sensor Operation	No

5.5.1 Result Summary

success	status="success"
failure	status="failure"
	message*=informative message describing failure
invalidId	status="invalidId"
	badFields={"sessionId"} (StringArray, §3.7)
lockHeldByAnother	status="lockHeldByAnother"
badValue	status="badValue"
	badFields={"sessionId"} (StringArray, §3.7)

5.5.2 Usage Notes

The *try lock* operation attempts to obtain the service lock. The word "try" is used to indicate that the call always returns immediately; it does not block until the lock is obtained. See §2.4.5 for detailed information about the WS-BD concurrency and locking model.

5.5.3 Unique Knowledge

As specified, the *try lock* cannot be used to provide or obtain knowledge about unique characteristics of a client or service.

5.5.4 Return Values Detail

The *try lock* operation *must* return a Result according to the following constraints.

5.5.4.1 Success

Status Value	success
Condition	The service was successfully locked to the provided session id.
Required Elements	status (Status, §3.10)
	the literal "success"
Optional Elements	None

Clients that hold the service lock are permitted to perform sensor operations (§2.4.5). By idempotency (§2.4.7), if a client already holds the lock, subsequent *try lock* operations *shall* also return `success`.

5.5.4.2 Failure

Status Value	`failure`
Condition	The service could not be locked to the provided session id.
Required Elements	`status` (Status, §3.10) the literal "`failure`"
Optional Elements	`message` (xs:string, [XSDPart2]) an informative description of the nature of the failure

Services *must* reserve a `failure` status to report system or internal failures and prevent the acquisition of the lock. Most *try lock* operations that do not succeed will not produce a `failure` status, but more likely a `lockHeldByAnother` status (See §5.5.4.4 for an example).

5.5.4.3 Invalid Id

Status Value	`invalidId`
Condition	The provided session id is not registered with the service.
Required Elements	`status` (Status, §3.10) the literal "`invalidId`" `badFields` (StringArray, §3.7) an array that contains the single field name, "`sessionId`"
Optional Elements	None

A session id is invalid if it does not correspond to an active registration. A session id *may* become unregistered from a service through explicit unregistration or triggered automatically by the service due to inactivity (§5.4.4.1).

See §5.1.2 for general information on how services *must* handle parameter failures.

5.5.4.4 Lock Held by Another

Status Value	`lockHeldByAnother`
Condition	The service could not be locked to the provided session id because the lock is held by another client.
Required Elements	`status` (Status, §3.10) the literal "`lockHeldByAnother`"
Optional Elements	None

EXAMPLE: The following sequence diagram illustrates a client that cannot obtain the lock (Client B) because it is held by another client (Client A).

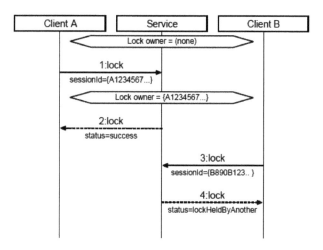

Figure 8. Example of a scenario yielding a lockHeldByAnother result.

5.5.4.5 Bad Value

Status Value	badValue
Condition	The provided session id is not a well-formed UUID.
Required Elements	status (Status, §3.10) 　　　　the literal "badValue" badFields (StringArray, §3.7) 　　　　an array that contains the single field name, "sessionId"
Optional Elements	None

See §5.1.2 for general information on how services *must* handle parameter failures.

5.6   Steal Lock

Description	Forcibly obtain the lock away from a peer client
URL Template	/lock/{sessionId}
HTTP Method	PUT
URL Parameters	{sessionId} (UUID, §3.2)
	Identity of the session requesting the service lock
Input Payload	None
Idempotent	Yes
Sensor Operation	No

5.6.1   Result Summary

success	status="success"
failure	status="failure"
	message*=informative message describing failure
invalidId	status="invalidId"
	badFields={"sessionId"} (StringArray, §3.7)
badValue	status="badValue"
	badFields={"sessionId"} (StringArray, §3.7)

5.6.2   Usage Notes

The _steal lock_ operation allows a client to forcibly obtain the lock away from another client that already holds the lock. The purpose of this operation is to prevent a client that experiences a fatal error from forever preventing another client access to the service, and therefore, the biometric sensor.

5.6.2.1   Avoid Lock Stealing

Developers and integrators _should_ endeavor to reserve lock stealing for exceptional circumstances—such as when a fatal error prevents a client from releasing a lock. Lock stealing _should not_ be used as the primary mechanism in which peer clients coordinate biometric sensor use.

5.6.2.2   Lock Stealing Prevention Period (LSPP)

To assist in coordinating access among clients and to prevent excessive lock stealing, a service _may_ trigger a time period that forbids lock stealing for each sensor operation. For convenience, this period of time will be referred to as the _lock stealing prevention period (LSPP)._

During the LSPP, all attempts to steal the service lock will fail. Consequently, if a client experiences a fatal failure during a sensor operation, then all peer clients need to wait until the service re-enables lock stealing.

All services _should_ implement a non-zero LSPP. The recommended time for the LSPP is on the order of 100 seconds. Services that enforce an LSPP _must_ start the LSPP immediately before sovereign sensor control is required. Conversely, services _should not_ enforce an LSPP unless absolutely necessary.

If a request provides an invalid `sessionId`, then the operation *should* return an `invalidId` status instead of a `failure`—this *must* be true regardless of the LSPP threshold and whether or not it has expired. A `failure` signifies that the state of the service is still within the LSPP threshold and the provided `sessionId` is valid.

A service *may* reinitiate a LSPP when an operation yields an undesirable result, such as `failure`. This would allow a client to attempt to resubmit the request or recover without worrying about whether or not the lock is still owned by the client's session.

An LSPP ends after a fixed amount of time has elapsed, unless another sensor operation restarts the LSPP. Services *should* keep the length of the LSPP fixed throughout the service's lifecycle. It is recognized, however, that there *may* be use cases in which a variable LSPP timespan is desirable or required. Regardless, when determining the appropriate timespan, implementers *should* carefully consider the tradeoffs between preventing excessive lock stealing, versus forcing all clients to wait until a service re-enables lock stealing.

5.6.2.3 Cancellation & (Lack of) Client Notification

Lock stealing *must* have no effect on any currently running sensor operations. It is possible that a client initiates a sensor operation, has its lock stolen away, yet the operation completes successfully. *Subsequent* sensor operations would yield a `lockNotHeld` status, which a client could use to indicate that their lock was stolen away from them. Services *should* be implemented such that the LSPP is longer than any sensor operation.

5.6.3   Unique Knowledge

As specified, the *steal lock* operation cannot be used to provide or obtain knowledge about unique characteristics of a client or service.

5.6.4   Return Values Detail

The *steal lock* operation *must* return a Result according to the following constraints.

5.6.4.1 Success

Status Value	success
Condition	The service was successfully locked to the provided session id.
Required Elements	status (Status, §3.10) the literal "success"
Optional Elements	None

See §2.4.5 for detailed information about the WS-BD concurrency and locking model. Cancellation *must* have no effect on pending sensor operations (§5.6.2.3).

5.6.4.2 Failure

Status Value	failure
Condition	The service could not be locked to the provided session id.
Required Elements	status (Status, §3.10) the literal "failure"

Optional Elements   message (xs:string, [XSDPart2])

an informative description of the nature of the failure

Most _steal lock_ operations that yield a failure status will do so because the service receives a lock stealing request during a lock stealing prevention period (§5.6.2.2). Services *must* also reserve a failure status for other non-LSPP failures that prevent the acquisition of the lock.

Implementers *may* choose to use the optional message field to provide more information to an end-user as to the specific reasons for the failure. However (as with all other failure status results), clients *must not* depend on any particular content to make this distinction.

5.6.4.3   Invalid Id

Status Value	invalidId
Condition	The provided session id is not registered with the service.
Required Elements	status (Status, §3.10) the literal "invalidId" badFields (StringArray, §3.7) an array that contains the single field name, "sessionId"
Optional Elements	None

A session id is invalid if it does not correspond to an active registration. A session id *may* become unregistered from a service through explicit unregistration or triggered automatically by the service due to inactivity (§5.4.4.1).

See §5.1.2 for general information on how services *must* handle parameter failures.

5.6.4.4   Bad Value

Status Value	badValue
Condition	The provided session id is not a well-formed UUID.
Required Elements	status (Status, §3.10) the literal "badValue" badFields (StringArray, §3.7) an array that contains the single field name, "sessionId"
Optional Elements	None

See §5.1.2 for general information on how services *must* handle parameter failures.

5.7   Unlock

Description	Release the service lock
URL Template	/lock/{sessionId}
HTTP Method	DELETE
URL Parameters	{sessionId} (UUID, §3.2) Identity of the session releasing the service lock
Input Payload	None
Idempotent	Yes
Sensor Operation	No

5.7.1   Result Summary

success	status="success"
failure	status="failure" message*=informative message describing failure
invalidId	status="invalidId" badFields={"sessionId"} (StringArray, §3.7)
badValue	status="badValue" badFields={"sessionId"} (StringArray, §3.7)

5.7.2   Usage Notes

The _unlock_ operation releases a service lock, making locking available to other clients.

See §2.4.5 for detailed information about the WS-BD concurrency and locking model.

5.7.3   Unique Knowledge

As specified, the _unlock_ operation cannot be used to provide or obtain knowledge about unique characteristics of a client or service.

5.7.4   Return Values Detail

The _steal lock_ operation _must_ return a Result according to the following constraints.

5.7.4.1   Success

Status Value	success
Condition	The service returned to an unlocked state.
Required Elements	status (Status, §3.10) the literal "success"
Optional Elements	None

Upon releasing the lock, a client is no longer permitted to perform any sensor operations (§2.4.5). By idempotency (§2.4.7), if a client already has released the lock, subsequent *unlock* operations *should* also return `success`.

5.7.4.2   Failure

Status Value	`failure`
Condition	The service could not be transitioned into an unlocked state.
Required Elements	`status` (Status, §3.10) the literal "`failure`"
Optional Elements	`message` (xs:string, [XSDPart2]) an informative description of the nature of the failure

Services *must* reserve a `failure` status to report system or internal failures and prevent the release of the service lock. The occurrence of *unlock* operations that fail is expected to be rare.

5.7.4.3   Invalid Id

Status Value	`invalidId`
Condition	The provided session id is not registered with the service.
Required Elements	`status` (Status, §3.10) the literal "`invalidId`" `badFields` (StringArray, §3.7) an array that contains the single field name, "`sessionId`"
Optional Elements	None

A session id is invalid if it does not correspond to an active registration. A session id *may* become unregistered from a service through explicit unregistration or triggered automatically by the service due to inactivity (§5.4.4.1).

See §5.1.2 for general information on how services *must* handle parameter failures.

5.7.4.4   Bad Value

Status Value	`badValue`
Condition	The provided session id is not a well-formed UUID.
Required Elements	`status` (Status, §3.10) the literal "`badValue`" `badFields` (StringArray, §3.7) an array that contains the single field name, "`sessionId`"
Optional Elements	None

See §5.1.2 for general information on how services *must* handle parameter failures.

5.8   Get Service Info

Description	Retrieve metadata about the service that does not depend on session-specific information, or sovereign control of the target biometric sensor
URL Template	/info
HTTP Method	GET
URL Parameters	None
Input Payload	None
Idempotent	Yes
Sensor Operation	No

5.8.1   Result Summary

success	status="success"
	metadata=dictionary containing service metadata (Dictionary, §3.3)
failure	status="failure"
	message*=informative message describing failure

5.8.2   Usage Notes

The *get service info* operation provides information about the service and target biometric sensor. This operation *must* return information that is both (a) independent of session, and (b) does not require sovereign biometric sensor control. In other words, services *must not* control the target biometric sensor during a *get service info* operation itself. Implementations *may* (and are encouraged to) use service startup time to query the biometric sensor directly to create a cache of information and capabilities for *get service info* operations. The service *should* keep a cache of sensor and service metadata to reduce the amount of operations that query the sensor as this can be a lengthy operation.

The *get service info* operation does *not* require that a client be registered with the service. Unlike other operations, it does *not* take a session id as a URL parameter.

See §4.1 for information about the metadata returned from this operation.

EXAMPLE: The following represents a 'raw' request to get the service's metadata.

```
GET http://10.0.0.8:8000/Service/info HTTP/1.1
Content-Type: application/xml
Host: 10.0.0.8:8000
```

EXAMPLE: The following is the 'raw' response from the above request. The metadata element of the result contains a Dictionary (§3.3) of parameter names and parameter information represented as a Parameter (§3.4).

```
HTTP/1.1 200 OK
Content-Length: 4244
Content-Type: application/xml; charset=utf-8
Server: Microsoft-HTTPAPI/2.0
Date: Tue, 03 Jan 2012 14:54:51 GMT
```

```
<result xmlns="urn:oid:2.16.840.1.101.3.9.3.1" xmlns:i="http://www.w3.org/2001/XMLSchema-instance">
  <status>success</status>

  <metadata>
    <item>
      <key>width</key>
      <value i:type="Parameter">
        <name>width</name>
        <q:type xmlns:q="urn:oid:2.16.840.1.101.3.9.3.1"
xmlns:a="http://www.w3.org/2001/XMLSchema">a:unsignedInt</q:type>
        <defaultValue i:type="a:int" xmlns:a="http://www.w3.org/2001/XMLSchema">800</defaultValue>
        <allowedValues>
          <allowedValue i:type="a:int" xmlns:a="http://www.w3.org/2001/XMLSchema">1280</allowedValue>
          <allowedValue i:type="a:int" xmlns:a="http://www.w3.org/2001/XMLSchema">960</allowedValue>
          <allowedValue i:type="a:int" xmlns:a="http://www.w3.org/2001/XMLSchema">800</allowedValue>
          <allowedValue i:type="a:int" xmlns:a="http://www.w3.org/2001/XMLSchema">640</allowedValue>
          <allowedValue i:type="a:int" xmlns:a="http://www.w3.org/2001/XMLSchema">424</allowedValue>
          <allowedValue i:type="a:int" xmlns:a="http://www.w3.org/2001/XMLSchema">416</allowedValue>
          <allowedValue i:type="a:int" xmlns:a="http://www.w3.org/2001/XMLSchema">352</allowedValue>
          <allowedValue i:type="a:int" xmlns:a="http://www.w3.org/2001/XMLSchema">320</allowedValue>
        </allowedValues>
      </value>
    </item>
    <item>
      <key>height</key>
      <value i:type="Parameter">
        <name>height</name>
        <q:type xmlns:q="urn:oid:2.16.840.1.101.3.9.3.1"
xmlns:a="http://www.w3.org/2001/XMLSchema">a:unsignedInt</q:type>
        <defaultValue i:type="a:int" xmlns:a="http://www.w3.org/2001/XMLSchema">600</defaultValue>
        <allowedValues>
          <allowedValue i:type="a:int" xmlns:a="http://www.w3.org/2001/XMLSchema">720</allowedValue>
          <allowedValue i:type="a:int" xmlns:a="http://www.w3.org/2001/XMLSchema">600</allowedValue>
          <allowedValue i:type="a:int" xmlns:a="http://www.w3.org/2001/XMLSchema">544</allowedValue>
          <allowedValue i:type="a:int" xmlns:a="http://www.w3.org/2001/XMLSchema">480</allowedValue>
          <allowedValue i:type="a:int" xmlns:a="http://www.w3.org/2001/XMLSchema">448</allowedValue>
          <allowedValue i:type="a:int" xmlns:a="http://www.w3.org/2001/XMLSchema">360</allowedValue>
          <allowedValue i:type="a:int" xmlns:a="http://www.w3.org/2001/XMLSchema">288</allowedValue>
          <allowedValue i:type="a:int" xmlns:a="http://www.w3.org/2001/XMLSchema">240</allowedValue>
          <allowedValue i:type="a:int" xmlns:a="http://www.w3.org/2001/XMLSchema">144</allowedValue>
          <allowedValue i:type="a:int" xmlns:a="http://www.w3.org/2001/XMLSchema">120</allowedValue>
        </allowedValues>
      </value>
    </item>
    <item>
      <key>frameRate</key>
      <value i:type="Parameter">
        <name>frameRate</name>
        <q:type xmlns:q="urn:oid:2.16.840.1.101.3.9.3.1"
xmlns:a="http://www.w3.org/2001/XMLSchema">a:unsignedInt</q:type>
        <defaultValue i:type="a:int" xmlns:a="http://www.w3.org/2001/XMLSchema">30</defaultValue>
        <allowedValues>
          <allowedValue i:type="a:int" xmlns:a="http://www.w3.org/2001/XMLSchema">30</allowedValue>
          <allowedValue i:type="a:int" xmlns:a="http://www.w3.org/2001/XMLSchema">15</allowedValue>
          <allowedValue i:type="a:int" xmlns:a="http://www.w3.org/2001/XMLSchema">10</allowedValue>
        </allowedValues>
      </value>
    </item>
    <item>
      <key>modality</key>
      <value i:type="Parameter">
        <name>modality</name>
        <q:type xmlns:q="urn:oid:2.16.840.1.101.3.9.3.1"
xmlns:a="http://www.w3.org/2001/XMLSchema">a:string</q:type>
        <readOnly>true</readOnly>
        <defaultValue i:type="a:string" xmlns:a="http://www.w3.org/2001/XMLSchema">face</defaultValue>
      </value>
    </item>
    <item>
      <key>submodality</key>
      <value i:type="Parameter">
        <name>submodality</name>
        <q:type xmlns:q="urn:oid:2.16.840.1.101.3.9.3.1"
xmlns:a="http://www.w3.org/2001/XMLSchema">a:string</q:type>
        <readOnly>true</readOnly>
        <defaultValue i:type="a:string" xmlns:a="http://www.w3.org/2001/XMLSchema">frontalFace</defaultValue>
      </value>
    </item>
```

```
    </metadata>
  </result>
```

5.8.3 Unique Knowledge

As specified, the _get service info_ can be used to obtain knowledge about unique characteristics of a service. Through _get service info_, a service _may_ expose implementation and/or service-specific configuration parameter names and values that are not defined in this specification (see Appendix A for further information on parameters).

5.8.4 Return Values Detail

The _get service info_ operation _must_ return a Result according to the following constraints.

5.8.4.1 Success

Status Value	success
Condition	The service provides service metadata
Required Elements	status (Status, §3.10) the literal "success" metadata (Dictionary, §3.3) information about the service metadata
Optional Elements	None

5.8.4.2 Failure

Status Value	failure
Condition	The service cannot provide service metadata
Required Elements	status (Status, §3.10) the literal "failure"
Optional Elements	message (xs:string, [XSDPart2]) an informative description of the nature of the failure

5.9   Initialize

Description	Initialize the target biometric sensor
URL Template	/initialize/{sessionId}
HTTP Method	POST
URL Parameters	{sessionId} (UUID, §3.2)
	Identity of the session requesting initialization
Input Payload	None
Idempotent	Yes
Sensor Operation	Yes

5.9.1   Result Summary

success	status="success"
failure	status="failure"
	message*=informative message describing failure
invalidId	status="invalidId"
	badFields={"sessionId"} (StringArray, §3.7)
canceled	status="canceled"
canceledWithSensorFailure	status="canceledWithSensorFailure"
sensorFailure	status="sensorFailure"
lockNotHeld	status="lockNotHeld"
lockHeldByAnother	status="lockHeldByAnother"
sensorBusy	status="sensorBusy"
sensorTimeout	status="sensorTimeout"
badValue	status="badValue"
	badFields={"sessionId"} (StringArray, §3.7)

5.9.2   Usage Notes

The *initialize* operation prepares the target biometric sensor for (other) sensor operations.

Some biometric sensors have no requirement for explicit initialization. In that case, the service *should* immediately return a success result.

Although not strictly necessary, services *should* directly map this operation to the initialization of the target biometric sensor, unless the service can reliably determine that the target biometric sensor is in a fully operational state. In other words, a service *may* decide to immediately return success if there is a reliable way to detect if the target biometric sensor is currently in an initialized state. This style of "short circuit" evaluation could reduce initialization times. However, a service that always initializes the target biometric sensor would enable the ability of a client to attempt a manual reset of a sensor that has entered a faulty state. This is particularly useful in physically separated service implementations where the connection between the target biometric sensor and the web service host may be less reliable than an integrated implementation.

5.9.3 Unique Knowledge

As specified, the *initialize* operation cannot be used to provide or obtain knowledge about unique characteristics of a client or service.

5.9.4 Return Values Detail

5.9.4.1 Success

Status Value	success
Condition	The service successfully initialized the target biometric sensor
Required Elements	status *must* be populated with the Status literal "success"
Optional Elements	None

5.9.4.2 Failure

Status Value	failure
Condition	The service experienced a fault that prevented successful initialization.
Required Elements	status (Status, §3.10) the literal "failure"
Optional Elements	message (xs:string, [XSDPart2]) an informative description of the nature of the failure

A failure status *must* only be used to report failures that occurred within the web service, not within the target biometric sensor (§5.9.4.5, §5.9.4.6)

5.9.4.3 Invalid Id

Status Value	invalidId
Condition	The provided session id is not registered with the service.
Required Elements	status (Status, §3.10) the literal "invalidId" badFields (StringArray, §3.7) an array that contains the single field name, "sessionId"
Optional Elements	None

A session id is invalid if it does not correspond to an active registration. A session id *may* become unregistered from a service through explicit unregistration or triggered automatically by the service due to inactivity (§5.4.4.1).

See §5.1.2 for general information on how services *must* handle parameter failures.

5.9.4.4 Canceled

Status Value	canceled
Condition	The initialization operation was interrupted by a cancellation request.
Required Elements	status (Status, §3.10) the literal "canceled"
Optional Elements	None

See §5.16.2.2 for information about what *may* trigger a cancellation.

5.9.4.5 Canceled with Sensor Failure

Status Value	canceledWithSensorFailure
Condition	The initialization operation was interrupted by a cancellation request and the target biometric sensor experienced a failure
Required Elements	status (Status, §3.10) the literal "canceledWithSensorFailure"
Optional Elements	message (xs:string, [XSDPart2]) an informative description of the nature of the failure

Services *must* return a canceledWithSensorFailure result if a cancellation request caused a failure within the target biometric sensor. Clients receiving this result may need to reattempt the initialization request to restore full functionality. See §5.16.2.2 for information about what *may* trigger a cancellation.

5.9.4.6 Sensor Failure

Status Value	sensorFailure
Condition	The initialization failed due to a failure within the target biometric sensor
Required Elements	status (Status, §3.10) the literal "sensorFailure"
Optional Elements	message (xs:string, [XSDPart2]) an informative description of the nature of the failure

A sensorFailure status *must* only be used to report failures that occurred within the target biometric sensor, not a failure within the web service (§5.9.4.2).

5.9.4.7 Lock Not Held

Status Value	lockNotHeld
Condition	Initialization could not be performed because the requesting client does not hold the lock
Required Elements	status (Status, §3.10) the literal "lockNotHeld"
Optional Elements	None

Sensor operations require that the requesting client holds the service lock.

5.9.4.8   Lock Held by Another

Status Value	lockHeldByAnother
Condition	Initialization could not be performed because the lock is held by another client.
Required Elements	status (Status, §3.10) the literal "lockHeldByAnother"
Optional Elements	None

5.9.4.9   Sensor Busy

Status Value	sensorBusy
Condition	Initialization could not be performed because the service is already performing a different sensor operation for the requesting client.
Required Elements	status (Status, §3.10) the literal "sensorBusy"
Optional Elements	None

5.9.4.10 Sensor Timeout

Status Value	sensorTimeout
Condition	Initialization could not be performed because the target biometric sensor took too long to complete the initialization request.
Required Elements	status (Status, §3.10) the literal "sensorTimeout"
Optional Elements	None

A service did not receive a timely response from the target biometric sensor. Note that this condition is distinct from the client's originating HTTP request, which *may* have its own, independent timeout. (See A.2 for information on how a client might determine timeouts.)

5.9.4.11 Bad Value

Status Value	badValue
Condition	The provided session id is not a well-formed UUID.

Required Elements	status (Status, §3.10)
	          the literal "badValue"
	
	badFields (StringArray, §3.7)
	          an array that contains the single field name, "sessionId"

Optional Elements	None

See §5.1.2 for general information on how services *must* handle parameter failures.

5.10 Get Configuration

Description	Retrieve metadata about the target biometric sensor's current configuration
URL Template	/configure/{sessionId}
HTTP Method	GET
URL Parameters	{sessionId} (UUID, §3.2)
	Identity of the session requesting the configuration
Input Payload	None
Idempotent	Yes
Sensor Operation	Yes

5.10.1 Result Summary

success	status="success"
	metadata=current configuration of the sensor (Dictionary, §3.3)
failure	status="failure"
	message*=informative message describing failure
invalidId	status="invalidId"
	badFields={"sessionId"} (StringArray, §3.7)
canceled	status="canceled"
canceledWithSensorFailure	status="canceledWithSensorFailure"
sensorFailure	status="sensorFailure"
lockNotHeld	status="lockNotHeld"
lockHeldByAnother	status="lockHeldByAnother"
initializationNeeded	status="initializationNeeded"
configurationNeeded	status="configurationNeeded"
sensorBusy	status="sensorBusy"
sensorTimeout	status="sensorTimeout"
badValue	status="badValue"
	badFields={"sessionId"} (StringArray, §3.7)

5.10.2 Usage Notes

The *get configuration* operation retrieves the service's current configuration.

EXAMPLE: The following represents a 'raw' request to retrieve the current configuration information of the service.

```
GET http://10.0.0.8:8000/Service/configure/d745cd19-facd-4f91-8774-aac5ca9766a2 HTTP/1.1
Content-Type: application/xml
Host: 10.0.0.8:8000
```

EXAMPLE: The following is the 'raw' response form the previous request. The `metadata` element in the result contains a Dictionary (§3.3) of parameter names and their respective values.

```
HTTP/1.1 200 OK
Content-Length: 554
Content-Type: application/xml; charset=utf-8
Server: Microsoft-HTTPAPI/2.0
Date: Tue, 03 Jan 2012 14:57:29 GMT

<result xmlns="urn:oid:2.16.840.1.101.3.9.3.1"
        xmlns:i="http://www.w3.org/2001/XMLSchema-instance">
  <status>success</status>
  <metadata>
    <item>
      <key>width</key>
      <value i:type="a:int" xmlns:a="http://www.w3.org/2001/XMLSchema">800</value>
    </item>
    <item>
      <key>height</key>
      <value i:type="a:int" xmlns:a="http://www.w3.org/2001/XMLSchema">600</value>
    </item>
    <item>
      <key>frameRate</key>
      <value i:type="a:int" xmlns:a="http://www.w3.org/2001/XMLSchema">15</value>
    </item>
  </metadata>
</result>
```

5.10.3 Unique Knowledge

As specified, the _get configuration_ can be used to obtain knowledge about unique characteristics of a service. Through _get configuration_, a service _may_ expose implementation and/or service-specific configuration parameter names and values that are not explicitly described in this document.

5.10.4 Return Values Detail

The _get configuration_ operation _must_ return a Result according to the following constraints.

5.10.4.1 Success

Status Value	success
Condition	The service provides the current configuration

Required Elements	status (Status, §3.10)
	        the literal "success"
	
	metadata (Dictionary, §3.3)
	        the target biometric sensor's current configuration

Optional Elements	None

See §4.2 for information regarding configurations.

5.10.4.2 Failure

Status Value	failure
Condition	The service cannot provide the current configuration due to service (not target biometric sensor) error.

Required Elements	status (Status, §3.10)
	the literal "failure"
Optional Elements	message (xs:string, [XSDPart2])
	an informative description of the nature of the failure

Services *must* only use this status to report failures that occur within the web service, not the target biometric sensor (see §5.10.4.5, §5.10.4.6).

5.10.4.3 Invalid Id

Status Value	invalidId
Condition	The provided session id is not registered with the service.
Required Elements	status (Status, §3.10)
	the literal "invalidId"
	badFields (StringArray, §3.7)
	an array that contains the single field name, "sessionId"
Optional Elements	None

A session id is invalid if it does not correspond to an active registration. A session id *may* become unregistered from a service through explicit unregistration or triggered automatically by the service due to inactivity (§5.4.4.1).

See §5.1.2 for general information on how services *must* handle parameter failures.

5.10.4.4 Canceled

Status Value	canceled
Condition	The *get configuration* operation was interrupted by a cancellation request.
Required Elements	status (Status, §3.10)
	the literal "canceled"
Optional Elements	None

See §5.16.2.2 for information about what *may* trigger a cancellation.

5.10.4.5 Canceled with Sensor Failure

Status Value	canceledWithSensorFailure
Condition	The *get configuration* operation was interrupted by a cancellation request during which the target biometric sensor experienced a failure
Required Elements	status (Status, §3.10)
	the literal "canceledWithSensorFailure"
Optional Elements	message (xs:string, [XSDPart2])
	an informative description of the nature of the failure

Services *must* return a `canceledWithSensorFailure` result if a cancellation request caused a failure within the target biometric sensor. Clients receiving this result *may* need to perform initialization to restore full functionality. See §5.16.2.2 for information about what *may* trigger a cancellation.

5.10.4.6 Sensor Failure

Status Value	`sensorFailure`
Condition	The configuration could not be queried due to a failure within the target biometric sensor.
Required Elements	`status` (Status, §3.10) the literal "`sensorFailure`"
Optional Elements	`message` (xs:string, [XSDPart2]) an informative description of the nature of the failure

A `sensorFailure` status *must* only be used to report failures that occurred within the target biometric sensor, not a failure within the web service (§5.9.4.2).

5.10.4.7 Lock Not Held

Status Value	`lockNotHeld`
Condition	The configuration could not be queried because the requesting client does not hold the lock.
Required Elements	`status` (Status, §3.10) the literal "`lockNotHeld`"
Optional Elements	None

Sensor operations require that the requesting client holds the service lock.

5.10.4.8 Lock Held by Another

Status Value	`lockHeldByAnother`
Condition	The configuration could not be queried because the lock is held by another client.
Required Elements	`status` (Status, §3.10) the literal "`lockHeldByAnother`"
Optional Elements	None

5.10.4.9 Initialization Needed

Status Value	`initializationNeeded`
Condition	The configuration could not be queried because the target biometric sensor has not been initialized.
Required Elements	`status` (Status, §3.10) the literal "`initializationNeeded`"
Optional Elements	None

Services *should* be able to provide the sensors configuration without initialization; however, this is not strictly necessary. Regardless, robust clients *should* assume that configuration will require initialization.

5.10.4.10   Configuration Needed

Status Value	configurationNeeded
Condition	The configuration could not be queried because the target biometric sensor has not been initialized.
Required Elements	status (Status, §3.10) the literal "configurationNeeded"
Optional Elements	None

Services *may* require configuration to be set before a configuration can be retrieved if a service does not provide a valid default configuration.

5.10.4.11   Sensor Busy

Status Value	sensorBusy
Condition	The configuration could not be queried because the service is already performing a different sensor operation for the requesting client.
Required Elements	status (Status, §3.10) the literal "sensorBusy"
Optional Elements	None

5.10.4.12   Sensor Timeout

Status Value	sensorTimeout
Condition	The configuration could not be queried because the target biometric sensor took too long to complete the request.
Required Elements	status (Status, §3.10) the literal "sensorTimeout"
Optional Elements	None

A service did not receive a timely response from the target biometric sensor. Note that this condition is distinct from the client's originating HTTP request, which *may* have its own, independent timeout. (See A.2 for information on how a client might determine timeouts.)

5.10.4.13   Bad Value

Status Value	badValue
Condition	The provided session id is not a well-formed UUID.

Required Elements	status (Status, §3.10)
	     the literal "badValue"
	badFields (StringArray, §3.7)
	     an array that contains the single field name, "sessionId"

Optional Elements   None

See §5.1.2 for general information on how services *must* handle parameter failures.

5.11   Set Configuration

Description	Set the target biometric sensor's configuration
URL Template	/configure/{sessionId}
HTTP Method	POST
URL Parameters	{sessionId} (UUID, §3.2) Identity of the session requesting the configuration
Input Payload	Desired sensor configuration (Dictionary, §3.3)
Idempotent	Yes
Sensor Operation	Yes

5.11.1   Result Summary

success	status="success"
failure	status="failure" message*=informative message describing failure
invalidId	status="invalidId" badFields={"sessionId"} (StringArray, §3.7)
canceled	status="canceled"
canceledWithSensorFailure	status="canceledWithSensorFailure"
sensorFailure	status="sensorFailure"
lockNotHeld	status="lockNotHeld"
lockHeldByAnother	status="lockHeldByAnother"
initializationNeeded	status="initializationNeeded"
sensorBusy	status="sensorBusy"
sensorTimeout	status="sensorTimeout"
unsupported	status="unsupported" badFields={field names} (StringArray, §3.7)
badValue	status="badValue" badFields={"sessionId"} (StringArray, §3.7) (or) status="badValue" badFields={field names} (StringArray, §3.7)
noSuchParameter	status="unsupported" badFields={field names} (StringArray, §3.7)

5.11.2   Usage Notes

The *set configuration* operation sets the configuration of a service's target biometric sensor.

5.11.2.1 Input Payload Information

The *set configuration* operation is the only operation that takes input within the body of the HTTP request. The desired configuration *must* be sent as a single Dictionary (§3.3) element named `configuration`. See §4.2 for information regarding configurations. See Appendix A for a complete XML Schema for this specification. The root element of the configuration data *must* conform to the following XML definition:

```
<xs:element name="configuration" type="wsbd:Dictionary" nillable="true"/>
```

EXAMPLE: The following represents a 'raw' request to configure a service at *http://10.0.0.8:8000/Sensor* such that `width=800`, `height=600`, and `frameRate=15`. (In this example, each `value` element contains fully qualified namespace information, although this is not necessary.)

```
POST http://10.0.0.8:8000/Service/configure/d745cd19-facd-4f91-8774-aac5ca9766a2 HTTP/1.1
Content-Type: application/xml
Host: 10.0.0.8:8000
Content-Length: 459
Expect: 100-continue

<configuration xmlns:i="http://www.w3.org/2001/XMLSchema-instance"
xmlns="urn:oid:2.16.840.1.101.3.9.3.1">
  <item>
    <key>width</key>
    <value xmlns:d3p1="http://www.w3.org/2001/XMLSchema" i:type="d3p1:int">800</value>
  </item>
  <item>
    <key>height</key>
    <value xmlns:d3p1="http://www.w3.org/2001/XMLSchema" i:type="d3p1:int">600</value>
  </item>
  <item>
    <key>frameRate</key>
    <value xmlns:d3p1="http://www.w3.org/2001/XMLSchema" i:type="d3p1:int">15</value>
  </item>
</configuration>
```

More information regarding the use of the `xmlns` attribute can be found in [XMLNS].

5.11.3 Unique Knowledge

The *set configuration* can be used to provide knowledge about unique characteristics to a service. Through *set configuration*, a client *may* provide implementation and/or service-specific parameter names and values that are not defined in this specification (see Appendix A for further information on parameters).

5.11.4 Return Values Detail

The *set configuration* operation *must* return a Result according to the following constraints.

5.11.4.1 Success

Status Value	success
Condition	The service was able to successfully set the full configuration
Required Elements	status (Status, §3.10) the literal "success"
Optional Elements	None

5.11.4.2 Failure

Status Value	failure
Condition	The service cannot set the desired configuration due to service (not target biometric sensor) error.
Required Elements	status (Status, §3.10) the literal "failure"
Optional Elements	message (xs:string, [XSDPart2]) an informative description of the nature of the failure

Services *must* only use this status to report failures that occur within the web service, not the target biometric sensor (see §5.11.4.5, §5.11.4.6).

5.11.4.3 Invalid Id

Status Value	invalidId
Condition	The provided session id is not registered with the service.
Required Elements	status (Status, §3.10) the literal "invalidId" badFields (StringArray, §3.7) an array that contains the single field name, "sessionId"
Optional Elements	None

A session id is invalid if it does not correspond to an active registration. A session id *may* become unregistered from a service through explicit unregistration or triggered automatically by the service due to inactivity (§5.4.4.1).

5.11.4.4 Canceled

Status Value	canceled
Condition	The *set configuration* operation was interrupted by a cancellation request.
Required Elements	status (Status, §3.10) the literal "canceled"
Optional Elements	None

See §5.16.2.2 for information about what *may* trigger a cancellation.

5.11.4.5 Canceled with Sensor Failure

Status Value	canceledWithSensorFailure
Condition	The *set configuration* operation was interrupted by a cancellation request during which the target biometric sensor experienced a failure
Required Elements	status (Status, §3.10) the literal "canceledWithSensorFailure"
Optional Elements	message (xs:string, [XSDPart2]) an informative description of the nature of the failure

Services *must* return a `canceledWithSensorFailure` result if a cancellation request caused a failure within the target biometric sensor. Clients receiving this result *may* need to perform initialization to restore full functionality. See §5.16.2.2 for information about what *may* trigger a cancellation.

5.11.4.6 Sensor Failure

Status Value	`sensorFailure`
Condition	The configuration could not be set due to a failure within the target biometric sensor.
Required Elements	`status` (Status, §3.10) the literal "`sensorFailure`"
Optional Elements	`message` (xs:string, [XSDPart2]) an informative description of the nature of the failure

A `sensorFailure` status *must* only be used to report failures that occurred within the target biometric sensor, not a failure within the web service (§5.11.4.2). Errors with the configuration itself *should* be reported via an `unsupported` (§5.11.4.12), `badValue` (§5.11.4.13), or `badValue` status (§5.11.4.14).

5.11.4.7 Lock Not Held

Status Value	`lockNotHeld`
Condition	The configuration could not be queried because the requesting client does not hold the lock.
Required Elements	`status` (Status, §3.10) the literal "`lockNotHeld`"
Optional Elements	None

Sensor operations require that the requesting client holds the service lock.

5.11.4.8 Lock Held by Another

Status Value	`lockHeldByAnother`
Condition	The configuration could not be set because the lock is held by another client.
Required Elements	`status` (Status, §3.10) the literal "`lockHeldByAnother`"
Optional Elements	None

5.11.4.9 Initialization Needed

Status Value	`initializationNeeded`
Condition	The configuration could not be set because the target biometric sensor has not been initialized.
Required Elements	`status` (Status, §3.10) the literal "`initializationNeeded`"
Optional Elements	None

Services *should* be able to set the configuration without initialization; however, this is not strictly necessary. Similarly, clients *should* assume that setting configuration will require initialization.

5.11.4.10   Sensor Busy

Status Value	sensorBusy
Condition	The configuration could not be set because the service is already performing a different sensor operation for the requesting client.
Required Elements	status (Status, §3.10) the literal "sensorBusy"
Optional Elements	None

5.11.4.11   Sensor Timeout

Status Value	sensorTimeout
Condition	The configuration could not be set because the target biometric sensor took too long to complete the request.
Required Elements	status (Status, §3.10) the literal "sensorTimeout"
Optional Elements	None

A service did not receive a timely response from the target biometric sensor. Note that this condition is distinct from the client's originating HTTP request, which *may* have its own, independent timeout. (See A.2 for information on how a client might determine timeouts.)

5.11.4.12   Unsupported

Status Value	unsupported
Condition	The requested configuration contains one or more values that are syntactically and semantically valid, but not supported by the service.
Required Elements	status (Status, §3.10) the literal "unsupported" badFields (StringArray, §3.7) an array that contains the field name(s) that corresponding to the unsupported value(s)
Optional Elements	None

Returning *multiple* fields allows a service to indicate that a particular *combination* of parameters is not supported by a service. See §5.1.2 for additional information on how services *must* handle parameter failures.

EXAMPLE: A WS-BD service utilizes a very basic off-the-shelf web camera with limited capabilities. This camera has three parameters that are all dependent on each other: ImageHeight, ImageWidth, and FrameRate. The respective allowed values for each parameter might look like: {240, 480, 600, 768}, {320, 640, 800, 1024}, and {5, 10, 15, 20, 30}. Configuring the sensor will return unsupported when the client tries to set ImageHeight=768, ImageWidth=1024, and FrameRate=30; this camera might not support capturing images of a higher resolution at a fast frame rate. Another example is configuring the sensor to use `ImageHeight=240` and `ImageWidth=1024`; as this is a very basic web camera, it might not support capturing images at this resolution. In both cases, the values provided for each parameter are individually valid but the overall validity is dependent on the combination of parameters

5.11.4.13   Bad Value

Status Value	`badValue`
Condition	Either: (a) The provided session id is not a well-formed UUID, or, (b) The requested configuration contains a parameter value that is either syntactically (e.g., an inappropriate data type) or semantically (e.g., a value outside of an acceptable range) invalid.

Required Elements	`status` (Status, §3.10)
	    the literal "`badValue`"
	
	`badFields` (StringArray, §3.7)
	    an array that contains either
	    (a) the single field name, "`sessionId`", or
	    (b) the field name(s) that contain invalid value(s)

Optional Elements	None

Notice that for the _set configuration_ operation, an invalid URL parameter _or_ one or more invalid input payload parameters can trigger a `badValue` status.

See §5.1.2 for general information on how services _must_ handle parameter failures.

5.11.4.14   No Such Parameter

Status Value	`noSuchParameter`
Condition	The requested configuration contains a parameter name that is not recognized by the service.

Required Elements	`status` (Status, §3.10)
	    the literal "`noSuchParameter`"
	
	`badFields` (StringArray, §3.7)
	    an array that contains the field name(s) that are not recognized by the service

Optional Elements	None

See §5.1.2 for general information on how services _must_ handle parameter failures.

5.12   Capture

Description	Capture biometric data
URL Template	/capture/{sessionId}
HTTP Method	POST
URL Parameters	{sessionId} (UUID, §3.2)
	Identity of the session requesting the configuration
Input Payload	None
Idempotent	No
Sensor Operation	Yes

5.12.1   Result Summary

success	status="success"
	captureIds={identifiers of captured data} (UuidArray, §3.8)
failure	status="failure"
	message*=informative message describing failure
invalidId	status="invalidId"
	badFields={"sessionId"} (StringArray, §3.7)
canceled	status="canceled"
canceledWithSensorFailure	status="canceledWithSensorFailure"
sensorFailure	status="sensorFailure"
lockNotHeld	status="lockNotHeld"
lockHeldByAnother	status="lockHeldByAnother"
initializationNeeded	status="initializationNeeded"
configurationNeeded	status="configurationNeeded"
sensorBusy	status="sensorBusy"
sensorTimeout	status="sensorTimeout"
badValue	status="badValue"
	badFields={"sessionId"} (StringArray, §3.7)

5.12.2   Usage Notes

The *capture* operation triggers biometric acquisition. On success, the operation returns one or more identifiers, or *capture id*s. Naturally, the *capture* operation is *not* idempotent. Each *capture* operation returns unique identifiers—each execution returning references that are particular to that capture. Clients then can retrieve the captured data itself by passing a *capture id* as a URL parameter to the *download* operation.

Multiple *capture ids* are supported to accommodate sensors that return collections of biometric data. For example, a multi-sensor array might save an image per sensor. A mixed-modality sensor might assign a different capture id for each modality.

IMPORTANT NOTE: The *capture* operation *may* include some post-acquisition processing. Although post-acquisition processing is directly tied to the *capture* operation, its effects are primarily on data transfer, and is therefore discussed in detail within the *download* operation documentation (§5.13.2.2)

5.12.2.1 Providing Timing Information

Depending on the sensor, a *capture* operation may take anywhere from milliseconds to tens of seconds to execute. (It is possible to have even longer running capture operations than this, but special accommodations *may* need to be made on the server and client side to compensate for typical HTTP timeouts.) By design, there is no explicit mechanism for a client to determine how long a capture operation will take. However, services can provide "hints" through capture timeout information (A.2.4), and clients can automatically adjust their own timeouts and behavior accordingly.

5.12.3 Unique Knowledge

As specified, the *capture* operation cannot be used to provide or obtain knowledge about unique characteristics of a client or service.

5.12.4 Return Values Detail

The *capture* operation *must* return a Result according to the following constraints.

5.12.4.1 Success

Status Value	`success`
Condition	The service successfully performed a biometric acquisition

Required Elements	`status` (Status, §3.10)
	        the literal `"success"`
	
	`captureIds` (UuidArray, §3.8)
	        one more UUIDs that uniquely identify the data acquired by the operation

Optional Elements	None

See the usage notes for *capture* (§5.12.2) and *download* (§5.13.2) for full detail.

5.12.4.2 Failure

Status Value	`failure`
Condition	The service cannot perform the capture due to a service (not target biometric sensor) error.
Required Elements	`status` (Status, §3.10) the literal `"failure"`
Optional Elements	`message` (xs:string, [XSDPart2]) an informative description of the nature of the failure

Services *must* only use this status to report failures that occur within the web service, not the target biometric sensor (see §5.12.4.5, §5.12.4.6). A service *may* fail at capture if there is not enough internal storage available to accommodate the captured data (§A.3).

5.12.4.3 Invalid Id

Status Value	invalidId
Condition	The provided session id is not registered with the service.

Required Elements	status (Status, §3.10)
	    the literal "invalidId"
	badFields (StringArray, §3.7)
	    an array that contains the single field name, "sessionId"

Optional Elements	None

A session id is invalid if it does not correspond to an active registration. A session id *may* become unregistered from a service through explicit unregistration or triggered automatically by the service due to inactivity (§5.4.4.1).

See §5.1.2 for general information on how services *must* handle parameter failures.

5.12.4.4 Canceled

Status Value	canceled
Condition	The *capture* operation was interrupted by a cancellation request.
Required Elements	status (Status, §3.10) the literal "canceled"
Optional Elements	None

See §5.16.2.2 for information about what *may* trigger a cancellation.

5.12.4.5 Canceled with Sensor Failure

Status Value	canceledWithSensorFailure
Condition	The *capture* operation was interrupted by a cancellation request during which the target biometric sensor experienced a failure
Required Elements	status (Status, §3.10) the literal "canceledWithSensorFailure"
Optional Elements	message (xs:string, [XSDPart2]) an informative description of the nature of the failure

Services *must* return a canceledWithSensorFailure result if a cancellation request caused a failure within the target biometric sensor. Clients receiving this result *may* need to perform initialization to restore full functionality. See §5.16.2.2 for information about what *may* trigger a cancellation.

5.12.4.6 Sensor Failure

Status Value	sensorFailure
Condition	The service could perform the capture due to a failure within the target biometric sensor.
Required Elements	status (Status, §3.10)

	the literal "sensorFailure"
Optional Elements	message (xs:string, [XSDPart2])
	an informative description of the nature of the failure

A sensorFailure status *must* only be used to report failures that occurred within the target biometric sensor, not a failure within the web service (§5.12.4.2).

5.12.4.7 Lock Not Held

Status Value	lockNotHeld
Condition	The service could not perform a capture because the requesting client does not hold the lock.
Required Elements	status (Status, §3.10)
	the literal "lockNotHeld"
Optional Elements	None

Sensor operations require that the requesting client holds the service lock.

5.12.4.8 Lock Held by Another

Status Value	lockHeldByAnother
Condition	The service could not perform a capture because the lock is held by another client.
Required Elements	status (Status, §3.10)
	the literal "lockHeldByAnother"
Optional Elements	None

5.12.4.9 Initialization Needed

Status Value	initializationNeeded
Condition	The service could not perform a capture because the target biometric sensor has not been initialized.
Required Elements	status (Status, §3.10)
	the literal "initializationNeeded"
Optional Elements	None

Services *should* be able perform capture without explicit initialization. However, the specification recognizes that this is not always possible, particularly for physically separated implementations. Regardless, for robustness, clients *should* assume that setting configuration will require initialization.

5.12.4.10   Configuration Needed

Status Value	configurationNeeded
Condition	The capture could not be set because the target biometric sensor has not been configured.
Required Elements	status (Status, §3.10)
	the literal "configurationNeeded"

Optional Elements   None

A service *should* offer a default configuration to allow capture to be performed without an explicit configuration. Regardless, for robustness, clients *should* assume that capture requires configuration.

5.12.4.11   Sensor Busy

Status Value	sensorBusy
Condition	The service could not perform a capture because the service is already performing a different sensor operation for the requesting client.
Required Elements	status (Status, §3.10) the literal "sensorBusy"
Optional Elements	None

5.12.4.12   Sensor Timeout

Status Value	sensorTimeout
Condition	The service could not perform a capture because the target biometric sensor took too long to complete the request.
Required Elements	status (Status, §3.10) the literal "sensorTimeout"
Optional Elements	None

A service did not receive a timely response from the target biometric sensor. Note that this condition is distinct from the client's originating HTTP request, which *may* have its own, independent timeout. (See §A.2 for information on how a client might determine timeouts.)

5.12.4.13   Bad Value

Status Value	badValue
Condition	The provided session id is not a well-formed UUID.
Required Elements	status (Status, §3.10) the literal "badValue" badFields (StringArray, §3.7) an array that contains the single field name, "sessionId"
Optional Elements	None

See §5.1.2 for general information on how services *must* handle parameter failures.

5.13 Download

Description	Download the captured biometric data
URL Template	/download/{captureId}
HTTP Method	GET
URL Parameters	{captureId} (UUID, §3.2) Identity of the captured data to download
Input Payload	None
Idempotent	Yes
Sensor Operation	No

5.13.1 Result Summary

success	status="success" metadata=sensor configuration at the time of capture (Dictionary, §3.3) sensorData=biometric data (xs:base64Binary)
failure	status="failure" message*=informative message describing failure
invalidId	status="invalidId" badFields={"captureId"} (StringArray, §3.7)
badValue	status="badValue" badFields={"captureId"} (StringArray, §3.7)
preparingDownload	status="preparingDownload"

5.13.2 Usage Notes

The *download* operation allows a client to retrieve biometric data acquired during a particular capture.

5.13.2.1 Capture and Download as Separate Operations

WS-BD decouples the acquisition operation (*capture*) from the data transfer (*download*) operation. This has two key benefits. First, it is a better fit for services that have post-acquisition processes. Second, it allows multiple clients to download the captured biometric data by exploiting the concurrent nature of HTTP. By making *download* a simple data transfer operation, service can handle multiple, concurrent downloads without requiring locking.

5.13.2.2 Services with Post-Acquisition Processing

A service does *not* need to make the captured data available immediately after capture; a service *may* have distinct acquisition and post-acquisition processes. The following are two examples of such services:

> **EXAMPLE:** A service exposing a fingerprint scanner also performs post processing on a fingerprint image—segmentation, quality assessment, and templatization.

EXAMPLE: A service exposes a digital camera in which the captured image is not immediately available after a photo is taken; the image may need to be downloaded from to the camera's internal storage or from the camera to the host computer (in a physically separated implementation). If the digital camera was unavailable for an operation due to a data transfer, a client requesting a sensor operation would receive a `sensorBusy` status.

The first method is to perform the post-processing within the _capture_ operation itself. I.e., _capture_ not only blocks for the acquisition to be performed, but also blocks for the post-processing—returning when the post-processing is complete. This type of capture is the easier of the two to both (a) implement on the client, and (b) use by a client.

EXAMPLE: Figure 9 illustrates an example of a _capture_ operation that includes post-processing. Once the post-processing is complete, capture ids are returned to the client.

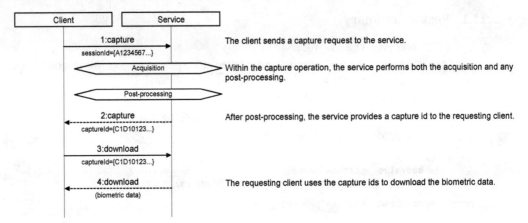

Figure 9. Including post-processing in the capture operation means downloads are immediately available when capture completes. Unless specified, the status of all returned operations is `success`.

In the second method, post-processing _may_ be performed by the web service _after_ the capture operation returns. Capture ids are still returned to the client, but are in an intermediate state. This exposes a window of time in which the capture is complete, but the biometric data is not yet ready for retrieval or download. Data-related operations (_download_, _get download info_, and _thrifty download_) performed within this window return a `preparingDownload` status to clients to indicate that the captured data is currently in an intermediate state—captured, but not yet ready for retrieval.

EXAMPLE: Figure 10 illustrates an example of a _capture_ operation with separate post-processing. Returning to the example of the fingerprint scanner that transforms a raw biometric sample into a template after acquisition, assume that the service performs templatization after capture returns. During post-processing, requests for the captured data return `preparingDownload`, but the sensor itself is available for another capture operation.

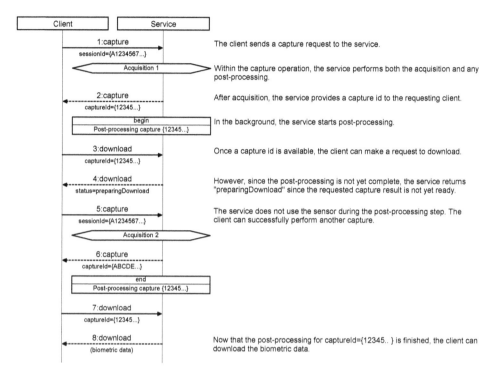

Figure 10. Example of capture with separate post-acquisition processing that does involve the target biometric sensor. Because the post-acquisition processing does not involve the target biometric sensor, it is available for sensor operations. Unless specified, the status of all returned operations is success.

Services with an independent post-processing step *should* perform the post-processing on an independent unit of execution (e.g., a separate thread, or process). However, post-processing *may* include a sensor operation, which would interfere with incoming sensor requests.

> **EXAMPLE**: Figure 11 illustrates another variation on a *capture* operation with separate post-processing. Return to the digital camera example, but assume that it is a physically separate implementation and capture operation returns immediately after acquisition. The service also has a post-acquisition process that downloads the image data from the camera to a computer. Like the previous example, during post-processing, requests for the captured data return preparingDownload. However, the sensor is *not* available for additional operations because the post-processing step requires complete control over the camera to transfer the images to the host machine: preparing them for download.

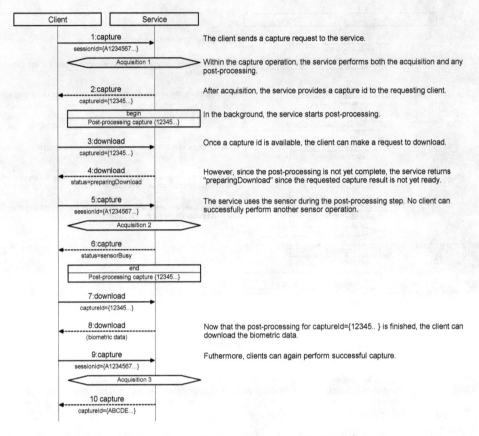

Figure 11. Example of capture with separate post-acquisition processing that does involve the target biometric sensor. Because the post-acquisition processing does not involve the target biometric sensor, it is available for sensor operations. Unless specified, the status of all returned operations is `success`.

Unless there is an advantage to doing so, when post-acquisition processing includes a sensor operation, implementers *should* avoid having a capture operation that returns directly after acquisition. In this case, even when the capture operation finishes, clients cannot perform a sensor operation until the post-acquisition processing is complete.

In general, implementers *should* try to combine both the acquisition and post-acquisition processing into one capture operation—particularly if the delay due to post-acquisition processing is either operationally acceptable or a relatively insignificant contributor to the combined time.

A *download* operation *must* return `failure` if the post-acquisition processing cannot be completed successfully. Such failures cannot be reflected in the originating *capture* operation —that operation has already returned successfully with capture ids. Services *must* eventually resolve all `preparingDownload` statuses to `success` or `failure`. Through *get service info*, a service can provide information to a client on how long to wait after capture until a `preparingDownload` is fully resolved.

5.13.2.3 Client Notification

A client that receives a `preparingDownload` *must* poll the service until the requested data becomes available. However, through *get service info*, a service can provide "hints" to a client on how long to wait after capture until data can be downloaded (§A.2.5)

5.13.3 **Unique Knowledge**

The *download* operation can be used to provide metadata, which *may* be unique to the service, through the `metadata` element. See §4 for information regarding metadata.

5.13.4 **Return Values Detail**

The *download* operation *must* return a Result according to the following constraints.

5.13.4.1 Success

Status Value	success
Condition	The service can provide the requested data

Required Elements	status (Status, §3.10)
	    the literal "success"
	
	metadata (Dictionary, §3.3)
	    sensor metadata as it was at the time of capture
	
	sensorData (xs:base64Binary, [XSDPart2])
	    the biometric data corresponding to the requested capture id, base-64 encoded

Optional Elements	None

A successful download *must* populate the Result with all of the following information:

1. The `status` element *must* be populated with the Status literal "success".
2. The `metadata` element *must* be populated with metadata of the biometric data and the configuration held by the target biometric sensor at the time of capture.
3. The `sensorData` element *must* contain the biometric data, base-64 encoded (xs:base64Binary), corresponding to the requested capture id.

See the usage notes for both *capture* (§5.12.2) and *download* (§5.13.2) for more detail regarding the conditions under which a service is permitted to accept or deny download requests.

5.13.4.2 Failure

Status Value	failure
Condition	The service cannot provide the requested data.
Required Elements	status (Status, §3.10) the literal "failure"
Optional Elements	message (xs:string, [XSDPart2]) an informative description of the nature of the failure

A service might not be able to provide the requested data due to failure in post-acquisition processing, a corrupted data store or other service or storage related failure.

5.13.4.3 Invalid Id

Status Value	invalidId
Condition	The provided capture id is not recognized by the service.

Required Elements	status (Status, §3.10)
	    the literal "invalidId"
	
	badFields (StringArray, §3.7)
	    an array that contains the single field name, "captureId"

Optional Elements	None

A capture id is invalid if it was not returned by a *capture* operation. A capture id *may* become unrecognized by the service automatically if the service automatically clears storage space to accommodate new captures (§A.3).

See §5.1.2 for general information on how services *must* handle parameter failures.

5.13.4.4 Bad Value

Status Value	badValue
Condition	The provided capture id is not a well-formed UUID.

Required Elements	status (Status, §3.10)
	    the literal "badValue"
	
	badFields (StringArray, §3.7)
	    an array that contains the single field name, "captureId"

Optional Elements	None

See §5.1.2 for general information on how services *must* handle parameter failures.

5.13.4.5 Preparing Download

Status Value	preparingDownload
Condition	The requested data cannot be provided because the service is currently performing a post-acquisition process—i.e., preparing it for download
Required Elements	status (Status, §3.10) the literal "preparingDownload"
Optional Elements	None

See the usage notes for both *capture* (§5.12.2) and *download* (§5.13.2) for full detail.

5.14   Get Download Info

Description	Get only the metadata associated with a particular capture
URL Template	/download/{captureId}/info
HTTP Method	GET
URL Parameters	{captureId} (UUID, §3.2) Identity of the captured data to query
Input Payload	Not applicable
Idempotent	Yes
Sensor Operation	No

5.14.1   Result Summary

success	status="success" metadata=sensor configuration at the time of capture
failure	status="failure" message*=informative message describing failure
invalidId	status="invalidId" badFields={"captureId"} (StringArray, §3.7)
badValue	status="badValue" badFields={"captureId"} (StringArray, §3.7)
preparingDownload	status="preparingDownload"

5.14.2   Usage Notes

Given the potential large size of some biometric data the _get download info_ operation provides clients with a way to get information about the biometric data without needing to transfer the biometric data itself. It is logically equivalent to the _download_ operation, but without any sensor data. Therefore, unless detailed otherwise, the usage notes for _download_ (§5.14.2) also apply to _get download info_.

5.14.3   Unique Knowledge

The _get download info_ operation can be used to provide metadata, which _may_ be unique to the service, through the metadata element. See §4 for information regarding metadata.

5.14.4   Return Values Detail

The _get download info_ operation _must_ return a Result according to the following constraints.

5.14.4.1 Success

Status Value	success
Condition	The service can provide the requested data
Required Elements	status (Status, §3.10)

	the literal `"success"`
	`metadata` (Dictionary, §3.3)
	the sensor's configuration as it was set at the time of capture
Optional Elements	None

A successful *get download info* operation returns all of the same information as a successful *download* operation (§5.13.4.1), but without the sensor data.

5.14.4.2 Failure

Status Value	`failure`
Condition	The service cannot provide the requested data.
Required Elements	`status` (Status, §3.10)
	the literal `"failure"`
Optional Elements	`message` (xs:string, [XSDPart2])
	an informative description of the nature of the failure

A service might not be able to provide the requested data due to failure in post-acquisition processing, a corrupted data store or other service or storage related failure.

5.14.4.3 Invalid Id

Status Value	`invalidId`
Condition	The provided capture id is not recognized by the service.
Required Elements	`status` (Status, §3.10)
	the literal `"invalidId"`
	`badFields` (StringArray, §3.7)
	an array that contains the single field name, `"captureId"`
Optional Elements	None

A capture id is invalid if it was not returned by a *capture* operation. A capture id *may* become unrecognized by the service automatically if the service automatically clears storage space to accommodate new captures (§A.3).

See §5.1.2 for general information on how services *must* handle parameter failures.

5.14.4.4 Bad Value

Status Value	`badValue`
Condition	The provided capture id is not a well-formed UUID.
Required Elements	`status` (Status, §3.10)
	the literal `"badValue"`
	`badFields` (StringArray, §3.7)
	an array that contains the single field name, `"captureId"`
Optional Elements	None

See §5.1.2 for general information on how services *must* handle parameter failures.

5.14.4.5 Preparing Download

Status Value	preparingDownload
Condition	The requested data cannot be provided because the service is currently performing a post-acquisition process—i.e., preparing it for download
Required Elements	status (Status, §3.10) the literal "preparingDownload"
Optional Elements	None

See the usage notes for both *capture* (§5.12.2) and *download* (§5.13.2) for full detail.

5.15 Thrifty Download

Description	Download a compact representation of the captured biometric data suitable for preview
URL Template	/download/{captureId}/{maxSize}
HTTP Method	GET
URL Parameters	{captureId} (UUID, §3.2) Identity of the captured data to download {maxSize} (xs:string, [XSDPart2]) Content-type dependent indicator of maximum permitted download size
Input Payload	None
Idempotent	Yes
Sensor Operation	No

5.15.1 Result Summary

success	status="success" metadata=minimal metadata describing the captured data (Dictionary, §3.3, §4.3.1) sensorData=biometric data (xs:base64Binary)
failure	status="failure" message*=informative message describing failure
invalidId	status="invalidId" badFields={"captureId"} (StringArray, §3.7)
badValue	status="badValue" badFields=either "captureId", "maxSize", or both (StringArray, §3.7)
unsupported	status="unsupported"
preparingDownload	status="preparingDownload"

5.15.2 Usage Notes

The *thrifty download* operation allows a client to retrieve a compact representation of the biometric data acquired during a particular capture. It is logically equivalent to the *download* operation, but provides a compact version of the sensor data. Therefore, unless detailed otherwise, the usage notes for *download* (§5.14.2) also apply to *get download info*.

The suitability of the *thrifty download* data as a biometric is implementation-dependent. For some applications, the compact representation may be suitable for use within a biometric algorithm; for others, it may only serve the purpose of preview.

For images, the maxSize parameter describes the maximum image width or height (in pixels) that the service *may* return; neither dimension *shall* exceed maxSize. It is expected that servers will dynamically scale the captured data to fulfill a client request. This is not strictly necessary, however, as long as the maximum size requirements are met.

For non-images, the default behavior is to return unsupported. It is *possible* to use URL parameter maxSize as general purpose parameter with implementation-dependent semantics. (See the next section for details.)

5.15.3 Unique Knowledge

The *thrifty download* operation can be used to provide knowledge about unique characteristics to a service. Through *thrifty download,* a service *may* (a) redefine the semantics of maxSize or (b) provide a data in a format that does not conform to the explicit types defined in this specification (see Appendix A for content types).

5.15.4 Return Values Detail

The *thrifty download* operation *must* return a Result according to the following constraints.

5.15.4.1 Success

Status Value	success
Condition	The service can provide the requested data
Required Elements	status (Status, §3.10) the literal "success"
	metadata (Dictionary, §3.3) minimal representation of sensor metadata as it was at the time of capture. See §4.3.1 for information regarding minimal metadata.
	sensorData (xs:base64Binary, [XSDPart2]) the biometric data corresponding to the requested capture id, base-64 encoded, scaled appropriately to the maxSize parameter.
Optional Elements	None

For increased efficiency, a successful *thrifty download* operation only returns the sensor data, and a subset of associated metadata. The metadata returned *should* be information that is absolutely essential to open or decode the returned sensor data.

5.15.4.2 Failure

Status Value	failure
Condition	The service cannot provide the requested data.
Required Elements	status (Status, §3.10) the literal "failure"
Optional Elements	message (xs:string, [XSDPart2]) an informative description of the nature of the failure

A service might not be able to provide the requested data due to a corrupted data store or other service or storage related failure.

5.15.4.3 Invalid Id

Status Value	invalidId

94

Condition	The provided capture id is not recognized by the service.
Required Elements	status (Status, §3.10) 　　the literal "invalidId" badFields (StringArray, §3.7) 　　an array that contains the single field name, "captureId"
Optional Elements	None

A capture id is invalid if it does not correspond to a _capture_ operation. A capture id _may_ become unrecognized by the service automatically if the service automatically clears storage space to accommodate new captures (§A.3).

See §5.1.2 for general information on how services _must_ handle parameter failures.

5.15.4.4 Bad Value

Status Value	badValue
Condition	The provided capture id is not a well-formed UUID.
Required Elements	status (Status, §3.10) 　　the literal "badValue" badFields (StringArray, §3.7) 　　an array that contains one or both of the following fields: 　　- "captureId" if the provided session id is not well-formed 　　- "maxSize" if the provided maxSize parameter is not well-formed
Optional Elements	None

See §5.1.2 for general information on how services _must_ handle parameter failures.

5.15.4.5 Unsupported

Status Value	unsupported
Condition	The service does not support thrifty download,
Required Elements	status (Status, §3.10) 　　the literal "unsupported"
Optional Elements	None

Services that capture biometrics that are not image-based _should_ return unsupported.

5.15.4.6 Preparing Download

Status Value	preparingDownload
Condition	The requested data cannot be provided because the service is currently performing a post-acquisition process—i.e., preparing it for download
Required Elements	status (Status, §3.10) 　　the literal "preparingDownload"
Optional Elements	None

95

Like _download_, the availability of _thrifty download_ data _may_ also be affected by the sequencing of post-acquisition processing. See §5.13.2.2 for detail.

5.16   Cancel

Description	Cancel the current sensor operation
URL Template	/cancel/{sessionId}
HTTP Method	POST
URL Parameters	{sessionId} (UUID, §3.2)
	Identity of the session requesting cancellation
Input Payload	None
Idempotent	Yes
Sensor Operation	Yes

5.16.1   Result Summary

success	status="success"
failure	status="failure"
	message*=informative message describing failure
invalidId	status="invalidId"
lockNotHeld	status="lockNotHeld"
lockHeldByAnother	status="lockHeldByAnother"
badValue	status="badValue"
	badFields={"sessionId"}

5.16.2   Usage Notes

The *cancel* operation stops any currently running sensor operation; it has no effect on non-sensor operations. If cancellation of an active sensor operation is successful, *cancel* operation receives a success result, while the canceled operation receives a canceled (or canceledWithSensorFailure) result. As long as the operation is canceled, the *cancel* operation itself receives a success result, regardless if cancellation caused a sensor failure. In other words, if cancellation caused a fault within the target biometric sensor, as long as the sensor operation has stopped running, the *cancel* operation is considered to be successful.

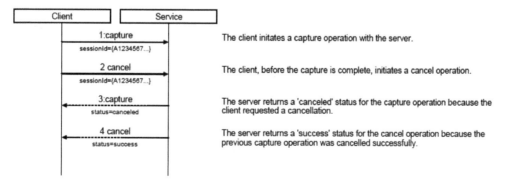

The client initates a capture operation with the server.

The client, before the capture is complete, initiates a cancel operation.

The server returns a 'canceled' status for the capture operation because the client requested a cancellation.

The server returns a 'success' status for the cancel operation because the previous capture operation was cancelled successfully.

Figure 12. Example sequence of events for a client initially requesting a capture followed by a cancellation request.

All services *must* provide cancellation for all sensor operations.

5.16.2.1 Canceling Non-Sensor Operations

Clients are responsible for canceling all non-sensor operations via client-side mechanisms only. Cancellation of sensor operations requires a separate service operation, since a service *may* need to "manually" interrupt a busy sensor. A service that had its client terminate a non-sensor operation would have no way to easily determine that a cancellation was requested.

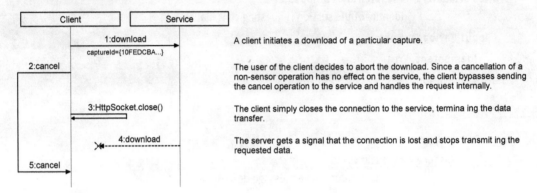

Figure 13. Cancellations of non-sensor operations do not require a cancel operation to be requested to the service. An example of this is where a client initiates then cancels a download operation.

5.16.2.2 Cancellation Triggers

Typically, the client that originates the sensor operation to be cancelled also initiates the cancellation request. Because WSBD operations are performed synchronously, cancellations are typically initiated on a separate unit of execution such as an independent thread or process.

Notice that the only requirement to perform cancellation is that the *requesting* client holds the service lock. It is *not* a requirement that the client that originates the sensor operation to be canceled also initiates the cancellation request. Therefore, it is *possible* that a client *may* cancel the sensor operation initiated by another client. This occurs if a peer client (a) manages to steal the service lock before the sensor operation is completed, or (b) is provided with the originating client's session id.

A service might also *self-initiate* cancellation. In normal operation, a service that does not receive a timely response from a target biometric sensor would return `sensorTimeout`. However, if the service's internal timeout mechanism fails, a service *may* initiate a cancel operation itself. Implementers *should* use this as a "last resort" compensating action.

In summary, clients *should* be designed to not expect to be able to match a cancelation notification to any specific request or operation.

5.16.3 Unique Knowledge

As specified, the *cancel* operation cannot be used to provide or obtain knowledge about unique characteristics of a client or service.

5.16.4 Return Values Detail

The *cancel* operation *must* return a Result according to the following constraints.

5.16.4.1 Success

Status Value	success
Condition	The service successfully canceled the sensor operation
Required Elements	status
	must be populated with the Status literal "success"
Optional Elements	None

See the usage notes for *capture* (§5.12.2) and *download* (§5.13.2) for full detail.

5.16.4.2 Failure

Status Value	failure
Condition	The service could not cancel the sensor operation
Required Elements	status (Status, §3.10)
	must be populated with the Status literal "failure"
Optional Elements	message (xs:string, [XSDPart2])
	an informative description of the nature of the failure

Services *should* try to return failure in a timely fashion—there is little advantage to a client if it receives the cancellation failure *after* the sensor operation to be canceled completes.

5.16.4.3 Invalid Id

Status Value	invalidId
Condition	The provided session id is not recognized by the service.
Required Elements	status (Status, §3.10)
	the literal "invalidId"
	badFields (StringArray, §3.7)
	an array that contains the single field name, "sessionId"
Optional Elements	None

A session id is invalid if it does not correspond to an active registration. A session id *may* become unregistered from a service through explicit unregistration or triggered automatically by the service due to inactivity (§5.4.4.1).

See §5.1.2 for general information on how services *must* handle parameter failures.

5.16.4.4 Lock Not Held

Status Value	lockNotHeld
Condition	The service could cancel the operation because the requesting client does not hold the lock.

Required Elements	status (Status, §3.10)
	the literal "lockNotHeld"
Optional Elements	None

Sensor operations require that the requesting client holds the service lock.

5.16.4.5 Lock Held by Another

Status Value	lockHeldByAnother
Condition	The service could not cancel the operation because the lock is held by another client.
Required Elements	status (Status, §3.10)
	the literal "lockHeldByAnother"
Optional Elements	None

5.16.4.6 Bad Value

Status Value	badValue
Condition	The provided session id is not a well-formed UUID.
Required Elements	status (Status, §3.10)
	the literal "badValue"
	badFields (StringArray, §3.7)
	an array that contains the single field name, "sessionId"
Optional Elements	None

See §5.1.2 for general information on how services *must* handle parameter failures.

Appendix A   Parameter Details

This appendix details the individual parameters available from a *get service info* operation. For each parameter, the following information is listed:

- The formal parameter name
- The expected data type of the parameter's value
- If a the service is required to implement the parameter

A.1   Connections

The following parameters describe how the service handles session lifetimes and registrations.

A.1.1   Last Updated

Formal Name	lastUpdated
Data Type	xs:dateTime [XSDPart2]
Required	Yes

This parameter provides a timestamp of when the service last *updated* the common info parameters (this parameter not withstanding). The timestamp *must* include time zone information. Implementers *should* expect clients to use this timestamp to detect if any cached values of the (other) common info parameters may have changed.

A.1.2   Inactivity Timeout

Formal Name	inactivityTimeout
Data Type	xs:nonNegativeInteger [XSDPart2]
Required	Yes

This parameter describes how long, in *seconds*, a session can be inactive before it *may* be automatically closed by the service. A value of '0' indicates that the service never drops sessions due to inactivity.

Inactivity time is measured *per session*. Services *must* measure it as the time elapsed between (a) the time at which a client initiated the session's most recent operation and (b) the current time. Services *must* only use the session id to determine a session's inactivity time. For example, a service does not maintain different inactivity timeouts for requests that use the same session id, but originate from two different IP addresses. Services *may* wait longer than the inactivity timeout to drop a session, but *must not* drop inactive sessions any sooner than the inactivityTimeout parameter indicates.

A.1.3   Maximum Concurrent Sessions

Formal Name	maximumConcurrentSessions
Data Type	xs:positiveInteger [XSDPart2]

Required	Yes

This parameter describes the maximum number of concurrent sessions a service can maintain. Upon startup, a service *must* have zero concurrent sessions. When a client registers successfully (§5.3), the service increases its count of concurrent sessions by one. After successful unregistration (§5.4), the service decreases its count of concurrent sessions by one   .

A.1.4   Least Recently Used (LRU) Sessions Automatically Dropped

Formal Name	autoDropLRUSessions
Data Type	xs:boolean [XSDPart2]
Required	Yes

This parameter describes whether or not the service automatically unregisters the least-recently-used session when the service has reached its maximum number of concurrent sessions. If *true*, then upon receiving a registration request, the service *may* drop the least-recently used session if the maximum number of concurrent sessions has already been reached. If *false*, then any registration request that would cause the service to exceed its maximum number of concurrent sessions results in failure. The service *shall not* drop a session that currently holds the lock unless the session's inactivity is outside of the inactivity timeout (§A.1.2) threshold.

A.2   Timeouts

Clients *should not* block indefinitely on any operation. However, since different services *may* differ significantly in the time they require to complete an operation, clients require a means to determine appropriate timeouts. The timeouts in this subsection describe how long a *service* waits until the service either returns sensorTimeout or initiates a service-side cancellation (§5.16.2.1). Services *may* wait longer than the times reported here, but, (under normal operations) *must not* report a sensorTimeout or initiate a cancellation before the reported time elapses. In other words, a client *should* be able to use these timeouts to help determine a reasonable upper bound on the time required for sensor operations.

Note that these timeouts do not include any round-trip and network delay—clients *should* add an additional window to accommodate delays unique to that particular client-server relationship.

A.2.1   Initialization Timeout

Formal Name	initializationTimeout
Data Type	xs:positiveInteger [XSDPart2]
Required	Yes

This parameter describes how long, in *milliseconds*, a service will wait for a target biometric sensor to perform initialization before it returns sensorTimeout (§5.9.4.10) or initiates a service-side cancellation (§5.16.2.1).

A.2.2   Get Configuration Timeout

Formal Name	getConfigurationTimeout

| Data Type | xs:positiveInteger [XSDPart2] |
| Required | Yes |

This parameter describes how long, in *milliseconds*, a service will wait for a target biometric sensor to retrieve its configuration before it returns sensorTimeout (§5.10.4.12) or initiates a service-side cancellation (§5.16.2.1).

A.2.3   Set Configuration Timeout

Formal Name	setConfigurationTimeout
Data Type	xs:positiveInteger [XSDPart2]
Required	Yes

This parameter describes how long, in *milliseconds*, a service will wait for a target biometric sensor to set its configuration before it returns sensorTimeout (§5.11.4.11) or initiates a service-side cancellation (§5.16.2.1).

A.2.4   Capture Timeout

Formal Name	captureTimeout
Data Type	xs:positiveInteger [XSDPart2]
Required	Yes

This parameter describes how long, in *milliseconds*, a service will wait for a target biometric sensor to perform biometric acquisition before it returns sensorTimeout (§5.11.4.11) or initiates a service-side cancellation (§5.16.2.1).

A.2.5   Post-Acquisition Processing Time

Formal Name	postAcquisitionProcessingTime
Data Type	xs:nonNegativeInteger [XSDPart2]
Required	Yes

This parameter describes an upper bound on how long, in *milliseconds*, a service takes to perform post-acquisition processing. A client *should not* expect to be able to download captured data *before* this time has elapsed. Conversely, this time also describes how long after a capture a server is permitted to return preparingDownload for the provided capture ids. A value of zero ('0') indicates that the service includes any post-acquisition processing within the capture operation or that no post-acquisition processing is performed.

A.2.6   Lock Stealing Prevention Period

Formal Name	lockStealingPreventionPeriod
Data Type	xs:nonNegativeInteger [XSDPart2]
Required	Yes

This parameter describes the length, in *milliseconds*, of the lock stealing prevention period (§5.6.2.2).

A.3   Storage

The following parameters describe how the service stores captured biometric data.

A.3.1   Maximum Storage Capacity

Formal Name	maximumStorageCapacity
Data Type	xs:positiveInteger [XSDPart2]
Required	Yes

This parameter describes how much data, in bytes, the service is capable of storing.

A.3.2   Least-Recently Used Capture Data Automatically Dropped

Formal Name	lruCaptureDataAutomaticallyDropped
Data Type	xs:boolean [XSDPart2]
Required	Yes

This parameter describes whether or not the service can automatically deletes the least-recently-used capture to stay within its maximum storage capacity. If *true*, the service *may* automatically delete the least-recently used biometric data to accommodate for new data. If *false*, then any operation that would require the service to exceed its storage capacity would fail.

A.4   Sensor

The following parameters describe information about the sensor and its supporting features

A.4.1   Modality

Formal Name	modality
Data Type	xs:string [XSDPart2]
Required	Yes

This parameter describes which modality or modalities are supported by the sensor.

The following table enumerates the list of modalities, as defined in [CBEFF2010], which provides the valid values for this field for currently identified modalities. Implementations are not limited to the following values, but *shall* use them if such modality is exposed. For example, if an implementation is exposing fingerprint capture capability, "Finger" *shall* be used. If an implementation is exposing an unlisted modality, it *may* use another value.

Modality Value	Description
Scent	Information about the scent left by a subject
DNA	Information about a subject's DNA
Ear	A subject's ear image

Face	An image of the subject's face, either in two or three dimensions
Finger	An image of one of more of the subject's fingerprints
Foot	An image of one or both of the subject's feet.
Vein	Information about a subject's vein pattern
HandGeometry	The geometry of an subject's hand
Iris	An image of one of both of the subject's irises
Retina	An image of one or both of the subject's retinas
Voice	Information about a subject's voice
Gait	Information about a subject's gait or ambulatory movement
Keystroke	Information about a subject's typing patterns
LipMovement	Information about a subject's lip movements
SignatureSign	Information about a subject's signature or handwriting

A.4.2   Submodality

Formal Name	submodality
Data Type	xs:string [XSDPart2]
Required	Yes

This parameter describes which submodalities are supported by the sensor.

Appendix B   Content Type Data

This appendix contains a catalog of content types for use in conformance profiles and parameters. When possible, the idenfied data formats *shall* be used.

B.1   General Type

application/xml	Extensible Markup Language (XML) [**XML**]
text/xml	Extensible Markup Language (XML) [**XML**]
text/plain	Plaintext [**RFC2046**]

B.2   Image Formats

Refer to [**CTypeImg**] for more information regarding a registered image type.

image/x-ms-bmp	Windows OS/2 Bitmap Graphics [**BMP**]
image/jpeg	Joint Photographics Experts Group [**JPEG**]
image/png	Portable Network Graphics [**PNG**]
image/tiff	Tagged Image File Format [**TIFF**]
image/x-wsq	Wavelet Scalar Quantization (WSQ) [**WSQ**]

B.3   Video Formats

Refer to [**CTypeVideo**] for more information regarding a registered video type.

video/h264	H.264 Video Compression [**H264**]
video/mpeg	Moving Pictures Experts Group [**MPEG**]

B.4   General Biometric Formats

x-biometric/x-ansi-nist-itl-2000	Information Technology: American National Standard for Information Systems—Data Format for the Interchange of Fingerprint, Facial, & Scar Mark & Tattoo (SMT) Information [**AN2K**]
x-biometric/x-ansi-nist-itl-2007	Information Technology: American National Standard for Information Systems—Data Format for the Interchange of Fingerprint, Facial, & Other Biometric Information – Part 1 [**AN2K7**]
x-biometric/x-ansi-nist-itl-2008	Information Technology: American National Standard for Information Systems—Data Format for the Interchange of Fingerprint, Facial, & Other Biometric Information – Part 2: XML Version [**AN2K8**]

x-biometric/x-ansi-nist-itl-2011	Information Technology: American National Standard for Information Systems—Data Format for the Interchange of Fingerprint, Facial & Other Biometric Information [AN2K11]
x-biometric/x-cbeff-2010	Common Biometric Exchange Formats Framework with Support for Additional Elements [CBEFF2010]

B.5   ISO / Modality-Specific Formats

x-biometric/x-iso-19794-2-05	Finger Minutiae Data [BDIF205]
x-biometric/x-iso-19794-3-06	Finger Pattern Spectral Data [BDIF306]
x-biometric/x-iso-19794-4-05	Finger Image Data [BDIF405]
x-biometric/x-iso-19794-5-05	Face Image Data [BDIF505]
x-biometric/x-iso-19794-6-05	Iris Image Data [BDIF605]
x-biometric/x-iso-19794-7-07	Signature/Sign Time Series Data [BDIF707]
x-biometric/x-iso-19794-8-06	Finger Pattern Skeletal Data [BDIF806]
x-biometric/x-iso-19794-9-07	Vascular Image Data [BDIF907]
x-biometric/x-iso-19794-10-07	Hand Geometry Silhouette Data [BDIF1007]

Appendix C   XML Schema

```xml
<?xml version="1.0"?>
<xs:schema xmlns:wsbd="urn:oid:2.16.840.1.101.3.9.3.1"
           xmlns:xs="http://www.w3.org/2001/XMLSchema"
           targetNamespace="urn:oid:2.16.840.1.101.3.9.3.1"
           elementFormDefault="qualified">

  <xs:element name="configuration" type="wsbd:Dictionary" nillable="true"/>
  <xs:element name="result" type="wsbd:Result" nillable="true"/>

  <xs:complexType name="Result">
    <xs:sequence>
      <xs:element name="status" type="wsbd:Status"/>
      <xs:element name="badFields" type="wsbd:StringArray" nillable="true" minOccurs="0"/>
      <xs:element name="captureIds" type="wsbd:UuidArray" nillable="true" minOccurs="0"/>
      <xs:element name="metadata" type="wsbd:Dictionary" nillable="true" minOccurs="0"/>
      <xs:element name="message" type="xs:string" nillable="true" minOccurs="0"/>
      <xs:element name="sensorData" type="xs:base64Binary" nillable="true" minOccurs="0"/>
      <xs:element name="sessionId" type="wsbd:UUID" nillable="true" minOccurs="0"/>
    </xs:sequence>
  </xs:complexType>

  <xs:simpleType name="UUID">
    <xs:restriction base="xs:string">
      <xs:pattern value="[\da-fA-F]{8}-[\da-fA-F]{4}-[\da-fA-F]{4}-[\da-fA-F]{4}-[\da-fA-F]{12}"/>
    </xs:restriction>
  </xs:simpleType>

  <xs:simpleType name="Status">
    <xs:restriction base="xs:string">
      <xs:enumeration value="success"/>
      <xs:enumeration value="failure"/>
      <xs:enumeration value="invalidId"/>
      <xs:enumeration value="canceled"/>
      <xs:enumeration value="canceledWithSensorFailure"/>
      <xs:enumeration value="sensorFailure"/>
      <xs:enumeration value="lockNotHeld"/>
      <xs:enumeration value="lockHeldByAnother"/>
      <xs:enumeration value="initializationNeeded"/>
      <xs:enumeration value="configurationNeeded"/>
      <xs:enumeration value="sensorBusy"/>
      <xs:enumeration value="sensorTimeout"/>
      <xs:enumeration value="unsupported"/>
      <xs:enumeration value="badValue"/>
      <xs:enumeration value="noSuchParamter"/>
      <xs:enumeration value="preparingDownload"/>
    </xs:restriction>
  </xs:simpleType>

  <xs:complexType name="Array">
    <xs:sequence>
      <xs:element name="element" type="xs:anyType" nillable="true" minOccurs="0" maxOccurs="unbounded"/>
    </xs:sequence>
  </xs:complexType>

  <xs:complexType name="StringArray">
    <xs:sequence>
      <xs:element name="element" type="xs:string" nillable="true" minOccurs="0" maxOccurs="unbounded"/>
    </xs:sequence>
  </xs:complexType>

  <xs:complexType name="UuidArray">
    <xs:sequence>
      <xs:element name="element" type="wsbd:UUID" nillable="true" minOccurs="0" maxOccurs="unbounded"/>
    </xs:sequence>
  </xs:complexType>

  <xs:complexType name="Dictionary">
    <xs:sequence>
      <xs:element name="item" minOccurs="0" maxOccurs="unbounded">
        <xs:complexType>
```

```xml
            <xs:sequence>
                <xs:element name="key" type="xs:string" nillable="true"/>

                <xs:element name="value" type="xs:anyType" nillable="true"/>
            </xs:sequence>
        </xs:complexType>
    </xs:element>
  </xs:sequence>
</xs:complexType>

<xs:complexType name="Parameter">
  <xs:sequence>
    <xs:element name="name" type="xs:string" nillable="true"/>
    <xs:element name="type" type="xs:QName" nillable="true"/>
    <xs:element name="readOnly" type="xs:boolean" minOccurs="0"/>
    <xs:element name="supportsMultiple" type="xs:boolean" minOccurs="0"/>
    <xs:element name="defaultValue" type="xs:anyType" nillable="true"/>
    <xs:element name="allowedValues" nillable="true" minOccurs="0">
      <xs:complexType>
        <xs:sequence>
          <xs:element name="allowedValue" type="xs:anyType" nillable="true" minOccurs="0" maxOccurs="unbounded"/>
        </xs:sequence>
      </xs:complexType>
    </xs:element>
  </xs:sequence>
</xs:complexType>

<xs:complexType name="Range">
  <xs:sequence>
    <xs:element name="minimum" type="xs:anyType" nillable="true" minOccurs="0"/>
    <xs:element name="maximum" type="xs:anyType" nillable="true" minOccurs="0"/>
    <xs:element name="minimumIsExclusive" type="xs:boolean" nillable="true" minOccurs="0"/>
        <xs:element name="maximumIsExclusive" type="xs:boolean" nillable="true" minOccurs="0"/>
  </xs:sequence>
</xs:complexType>

<xs:complexType name="Resolution">
  <xs:sequence>
    <xs:element name="width" type="xs:decimal"/>
    <xs:element name="height" type="xs:decimal"/>
    <xs:element name="unit" type="xs:string" nillable="true" minOccurs="0"/>
  </xs:sequence>
</xs:complexType>
</xs:schema>
```

Appendix D   Acknowledgments

The authors thank the following individuals and organizations for their participation in the creation of this specification.

Biometric Standards Working Group, Department of Defense
Michael Albright, Vision and Security Technology Laboratory, University of Colorado at Colorado Springs
Senaka Balasuriya, SolidBase Consulting
Terrance Boult, Vision and Security Technology Laboratory, University of Colorado at Colorado Springs
Leslie Collica, Information Technology Laboratory, National Institute of Standards and Technology
Tod Companion, Science & Technology Directorate, Department of Homeland Security
Bert Coursey, Science & Technology Directorate, Department of Homeland Security
Nick Crawford, Government Printing Office
Donna Dodson, Information Technology Laboratory, National Institute of Standards and Technology
Valerie Evanoff, Biometric Center of Excellence, Federal Bureau of Investigation
Rhonda Farrell, Booz Allen Hamilton
Michael Garris, Information Technology Laboratory, National Institute of Standards and Technology
Phillip Griffin, Booz Allen Hamilton
Dwayne Hill, Biometric Standards Working Group, Department of Defense
Rick Lazarick, Computer Sciences Corporation
John Manzo, Biometric Center of Excellence, Federal Bureau of Investigation
Charles Romine, Information Technology Laboratory, National Institute of Standards and Technology
James St. Pierre, Information Technology Laboratory, National Institute of Standards and Technology
Scott Swann, Federal Bureau of Investigation
Ashit Talukder, Information Technology Laboratory, National Institute of Standards and Technology
Cathy Tilton, Daon Inc.
Ryan Triplett, Biometric Standards Working Group, Department of Defense
Bradford Wing, Information Technology Laboratory, National Institute of Standards and Technology

Appendix E   Revision History

Release	Changeset
Draft 0 January 2011	Initial release. Operations and data types are well defined, but detailed documentation is not yet complete. Appendixes (metadata, conformance, and security profiles) are not yet written.
Draft 1 March 2011	Second release. Made significant improvements based on public comment. Removed 'Detailed Info' and augmented 'Get Content Type' into 'Get Download Info.' Detailed operation documentation is complete, but appendixes still need work.
Draft 2 August 2011	Third release. Made significant improvements based on comments provided by Department of Defense. Added section related to 'Metadata'. Modified WsbdResult to combine common fields into a single metadata field. Added WsbdRange and WsbdParameter types to the data dictionary.
Draft 3 October 2011	Fourth release. Removed Wsbd prefix from data elements and updated affected examples. Modified Range type to include value, now RangeOrValue.
Draft 4 December 2011	Fifth release. Candidate for first official release. Design philosophy, data dictionary, web service operations, and metadata are updated.
Version 1 March 2012	First official version. Updated formatting, fixed typos, and added some explaintory sections (such as the sequence diagram anatomy).

Document generated: 27 March 2012 14:41

www.ingramcontent.com/pod-product-compliance
Lightning Source LLC
Chambersburg PA
CBHW080428060326
40689CB00019B/4425